CULTURES OF THE WORLD
Cameroon

Cavendish Square
New York

Published in 2020 by Cavendish Square Publishing, LLC
243 5th Avenue, Suite 136, New York, NY 10016
Copyright © 2020 by Cavendish Square Publishing, LLC

Third Edition

Library of Congress Cataloging-in-Publication Data

Names: Nevins, Debbie, author. | Sheehan, Sean, 1951- author. | Elias,
   Josie, author.
Title: Cameroon / Debbie Nevins, [Sean Sheehan and Josie Elias].
Other titles: Cultures of the world (third edition)
Description: Third edition. | New York : Cavendish Square Publishing, 2020.
   | Series: Cultures of the world, third edition | "Writers, Sean Sheehan
   and Josie Elias; Debbie Nevins, third edition."--Title page verso. |
   Includes bibliographical references and index. | Audience: Ages 13 |
   Audience: Grades 7-9
Identifiers: LCCN 2019029242 (print) | LCCN 2019029243 (ebook) | ISBN
   9781502650702 (library binding) | ISBN 9781502650719 (ebook)
Subjects: LCSH: Cameroon--Juvenile literature.
Classification: LCC DT564 .S48 2020 (print) | LCC DT564 (ebook) | DDC
   967.11--dc23
LC record available at https://lccn.loc.gov/2019029242
LC ebook record available at https://lccn.loc.gov/2019029243

Writers, Sean Sheehan and Josie Elias; Debbie Nevins, third edition
Editorial Director, third edition: Katherine Kawa
Editor, third edition: Debbie Nevins
Art Director, third edition: Andrea Davison-Bartolotta
Designer, third edition: Jessica Nevins
Production Manager, third edition: Rachel Rising
Picture Researcher, third edition: Jessica Nevins

The photographs in this book are used with the permission of: Cover georgeclerk/E+/Getty Images; pp. 1, 18, 54, 66, 67, 103 Homo Cosmicos/Shutterstock.com; pp. 3, 56, 58 edeantoine/Shutterstock.com; pp. 5, 77, 79, 100, 120 akturer/Shutterstock.com; p. 6 REINNIER KAZE/AFP/Getty Images; p. 8 STR/AFP/Getty Images; p. 9 FABRICE COFFRINI/AFP/Getty Images; p. 10 Artindo/Shutterstock.com; p. 12 Adamawa/Shutterstock.com; p. 13 DeAgostini/Getty Images; p. 14 Michal Szymanski/Shutterstock.com; pp. 15, 73, 123 Fabian Plock/Shutterstock.com; p. 16 Matthias G. Ziegler/Shutterstock.com; p. 17 Radu Bercan/Shutterstock.com; p. 21 Universal History Archive/Universal Images Group via Getty Images; p. 24 Everett Historical/Shutterstock.com; p. 27 Roke/Wikimedia Commons/File:Cameroon boundary changes.PNG/CC BY-SA 3.0; pp. 29, 36 -/AFP/Getty Images; p. 30 Michel BARET/Gamma-Rapho via Getty Images; p. 32 THOMAS SAMSON/AFP/Getty Images; p. 34 Jiri Flogel/Shutterstock.com; p. 38 HAKON MOSVOLD LARSEN/AFP/Getty Images; p. 39 Daniel SIMON/Gamma-Rapho via Getty Images; p. 40 Lintao Zhang/Getty Images; p. 41 SEYLLOU/AFP/Getty Images; p. 43 mtcurado/iStock Unreleased/Getty Images; pp. 46, 62, 126 Scarabea/Shutterstock.com; p. 49 smspsy/Shutterstock.com; p. 50 Universal Images Group via Getty Images; p. 51 Avalon/Universal Images Group via Getty Images; p. 52 Kelsey M Weber/Shutterstock.com; p. 59 Kit Korzun/Shutterstock.com; p. 61 Robin Nieuwenkamp/Shutterstock.com; pp. 64, 105 Sylvie Bouchard/Shutterstock.com; p. 68 H. Christoph/ullstein bild via Getty Images; pp. 70, 74, 127 davide bonaldo/Shutterstock.com; p. 72 StreetVJ/Shutterstock.com; p. 75 STEFAN HEUNIS/AFP/Getty Images; p. 78 CHRISTOPHE SIMON/AFP/Getty Images; p. 82 NABILA EL HADAD/AFP/Getty Images; p. 85 Eye Ubiquitous/Universal Images Group via Getty Images; p. 86 Eric TRAVERS/Gamma-Rapho via Getty Images; pp. 87, 92 Yvan Travert/Photononstop/Getty Images Plus; p. 89 Ali Yildiz/Anadolu Agency/Getty Images; p. 90 STR/AFP/Getty Images; p. 93 Giles Clarke/UNOCHA via Getty Images; p. 96 Maurice ASCANI/Gamma-Rapho via Getty Images; p. 98 POZZO DI BORGO Thomas/Shutterstock.com; p. 101 Cultura RM Exclusive/Philip Lee Harvey/Cultura Exclusive/Getty Images Plus; p. 104 Thierry Chesnot/Getty Images; p. 106 Leonardo Cendamo/Getty Images; p. 108 MissHibiscus/iStock/Getty Images Plus; p. 114 Jean Pierre Kepseu/Anadolu Agency/Getty Images; p. 118 Mahaux Charles/AGF/Universal Images Group via Getty Images; p. 122 ASAEL Anthony/hemis.fr/Getty Images Plus; p. 125 Yapasphoto StefClement/Shutterstock.com; p. 128 Ammonite/Shutterstock.com; p. 130 Fanfo/Shutterstock.com; p. 131 Alucardion/Shutterstock.com; p. 137 T. Lesia/Shutterstock.com.

Printed in the United States of America

CONTENTS

CAMEROON TODAY

A **CATCHPHRASE OFTEN USED TO DESCRIBE THE AFRICAN NATION** of Cameroon is "all of Africa in one country." From its active volcanoes, tropical rain forests, grassy savannas, and deserts, to its rushing waterfalls and sandy ocean beaches, Cameroon's diversity of terrain and climate reflects the continent in miniature. The country is also home to many of Africa's most iconic animals—elephants, chimpanzees, apes, gorillas, rhinoceroses, hippopotamuses, giraffes, lions, antelope, cheetahs, and many others. With such an array of wildlife and natural beauty, Cameroon is something of a tourist destination, but its potential is far from realized. The reason lies amid the country's multitude of challenges—political, economic, and cultural.

The Republic of Cameroon lies in equatorial central-west Africa. It is a tropical central African nation on the Gulf of Guinea. From its west coast on the Gulf to the heart of the African continent and north to Lake Chad, its area is nearly 184,000 square miles (475,440 square kilometers), slightly larger than the state of California.

The present country was formed in 1961 when the former French Cameroon and a part of British Cameroon merged. This land is home to an astonishing variety of cultural groups, numbering over 250, who are gradually casting off a colonial heritage acquired in long periods of foreign rule by France and Britain.

Cameroon has generally enjoyed stability, which has permitted the development of roads, railways, and agriculture, as well as a petroleum industry. It is one of the few countries in Africa that has managed to evolve from a colony to an independent nation with very little bloodshed—at least up to this point.

However, recent developments are shaking its equilibrium. Cameroon is facing several simultaneous crises, and its government has so far been unable to meet the challenges. For one thing, Cameroon is feeling the effects of turmoil in some of its neighbors. In 2019, according to the Office of the United Nations High Commissioner for Refugees (UNHCR), Cameroon hosted a population of refugees and asylum seekers of approximately 1,305,000. Of these, some

Yaouba Hamadou (*front center*), a thirteen-year-old refugee from the Central African Republic, arrives at a refugee camp in Cameroon, escorted by the International Committee of the Red Cross.

285,200 were from the Central African Republic, 105,000 were from Nigeria, and 1,600 were from Chad.

The numbers have long been growing. The Central African Republic has been involved in a civil war since 2012, and refugees have sought shelter by crossing the Bombe River into Cameroon. From Chad and Nigeria, refugees fleeing the Boko Haram jihadist insurgents have also escaped to Cameroon. Some of these displaced people end up living for years in substandard conditions in camps, in local towns, or simply in the wild, where they have inadequate food, water, sanitation, and medical care. Far from being a wealthy nation, Cameroon cannot afford to care for these refugees. The three provinces hosting these refugees—the Far North, Adamawa, and East regions—also have the highest poverty levels in the country. International aid organizations struggle to help, as they themselves have insufficient funds and supplies.

Ironically, as Nigerian refugees flee to Cameroon, Cameroonians have also fled to Nigeria. Both groups are on the run for the same reason—to escape Boko Haram. Since 2009, this terrorist group, officially named the Islamic State in West Africa (ISWA), has led an armed campaign to establish an Islamic caliphate in Nigeria's northeast. The insurgents have increasingly encroached into Cameroon, finding recruits and launching assaults on civilians and troops alike.

A second crisis is a homegrown problem. A nation glued together from previous English and French colonies, Cameroon has two official languages—English and French—but the French-speaking part of the nation is dominant, with 80 percent of the population. This dominance spills over into political advantage as well, and Anglophones complain of being marginalized. In addition, the separate language regions have two different education and justice systems. Recent attempts by the predominately French government to unify the systems added to existing tensions. Conflicts have turned violent in recent years, leading to an Anglophone separatist insurgency bent on secession from the country. Clashes between the separatists and government troops have prompted conditions close to civil war. The violence has spurred new waves of refugees.

It has also cost the country economically. This was demonstrated by the events of the Africa Cup of Nations 2019, which was to take place in Cameroon's capital city of Yaoundé. Being a nation of avid football (soccer) fans, Cameroon was thrilled to be hosting the prestigious championship tournament—its first time since 1972. It was well into building stadiums and other buildings for the event when the organizers chose to relocate it to Egypt. Why? Among other reasons, there were security concerns relating to Cameroon's Anglophone unrest.

As these crises unfold, the leadership of the country is called into question, and therein lie a host of troubles. Cameroon has been governed by the same man since 1982. President Paul Biya, born in 1933, has won reelection multiple times. In fact, the country's constitution was changed to enable him to run indefinitely, which was accomplished amid much controversy in 2008. As he has won recent elections by ever-larger landslides, critics have alleged the elections were fraudulent. Following his victory in the 2018 election, ForeignPolicy.com, a media organization devoted to covering global affairs, called it a "farce" and a "master class in fake democracy."

Biya's government has been called one of the most corrupt in the world. In 2018, the anti-corruption organization Transparency International rated Cameroon number 152 out of 180 nations, a dismal score in which the highest numbers were the most corrupt. In fact, corruption seems to permeate Cameroonian life. Even desperate refugees trying to cross the border complain of being routinely asked for bribes by Cameroonian troops.

Biya's reputation extends far beyond his own realm. When, in June 2019, the president visited Geneva, Switzerland, as he often has, he was met with violent protests. One Swiss member of parliament even drew up a petition to oust Biya from the country. Indeed, Biya has been accused of essentially ruling his country from the Hotel Intercontinental in Geneva, where he is frequently in residence, at a cost to the Cameroonian taxpayers of about $40,000 per day.

Under this president—or some would say dictator—human rights abuses have surged. In its 2019 Freedom in the World Index, the human rights organization Freedom House ranked Cameroon "not free." The report expounded on the multiple examples of government obstruction of political and civil liberties in the country and noted that the situation was becoming increasingly dire.

Swiss police try to protect a woman wearing a dress adorned with pictures of President Paul Biya as she is attacked by anti-Biya protesters in Geneva, Switzerland, on June 29, 2019. Cameroonian nationals living in Europe were protesting outside the luxury hotel where Biya was staying, as large numbers of police, many in riot gear, were posted on the scene.

GEOGRAPHY

Cameroon, positioned on the interior corner of Africa's Atlantic shoreline, appears in the darker tone on this map of the African continent.

CAMEROON IS SOMETIMES CALLED the "hinge of Africa" because of its location at the juncture of western and southern Africa. The country is tucked into the corner where the continent's Atlantic coastline—under the enormous bulge of the West African landmass—abruptly changes direction from west—east to north—south. The expanse of tropical ocean in that great bend is called the Gulf of Guinea. From its coast on the gulf, Cameroon extends inland, with an arm reaching north to Lake Chad. In total land area—183,586 square miles (475,440 sq km)—the country is slightly larger than California.

Cameroon shares its borders with a number of other countries—Nigeria to the northwest; Chad to the northeast; the Central African Republic to the east; and Equatorial Guinea, Gabon, and the Republic of the Congo to the south. Cameroon's watery borders are the Atlantic Ocean to the southwest and Lake Chad in its northernmost frontier.

1

Mount Cameroon, a treeless, active volcano with an elevation of 13,250 feet (4,040 meters), is the highest peak in Cameroon. Located near the coast of the Gulf of Guinea, it's the fourth-highest mountain on the African continent.

FOUR REGIONS

Cameroon has four main geographical regions: the Lake Chad Basin, the central plateaus, the western highlands, and the coastal lowlands.

The Lake Chad Basin, at the northern tip of Cameroon, depends on the Logone River and its rich fishing grounds, which provide the main source of food for the people in the area. The Logone River flows for 240 miles (386 kilometers) northwest to N'Djamena in Chad, then merges with the Chari River.

The most important feature of north-central Cameroon is the volcanic upland of the grassy, rugged Adamawa Plateau, which extends into southeastern Nigeria. The plateau forms the main watershed of Cameroon and has a major influence on the country's weather patterns. It was named after Modibo Adama, a nineteenth-century Fulani scholar and warrior who founded a state in the area. From the plateau, which has an average elevation of 3,600 feet (1,097 m), a number of major rivers flow into Lake Chad, the Congo Basin, the Gulf of Guinea, and the Niger River in Nigeria. The most important of these rivers is the Benue (Bénoué), a 673-mile-long (1,083 km) tributary of the Niger River. The Benue descends more than 2,000 feet (610 m) over many rapids. Along

The Benue River flows close to the Nigeria-Cameroon border.

DISAPPEARING LAKE CHAD

Lake Chad is located at the northernmost tip of Cameroon. It extends into the far west of Chad, the northeast of Nigeria, and part of southeastern Niger. Essentially, the lake covers the region where those countries would otherwise converge. It was once Africa's largest water reservoir in the sub-Saharan region, covering an area of about 10,039 square miles (26,000 sq km), about the size of the US state of Maryland.

However, from 1963 to 1998, the lake shrank by almost 95 percent, wreaking havoc on the lives of the thirty million people who depended on it. Villages that were once lakeside are now many miles from the shore.

This aerial view shows a dried-up region of Lake Chad. When the lake level rises, these rocky features are surrounded by water.

Lake Chad's water is used for drinking, bathing, irrigation, and fishing. The lake not only supports marine life but also migrating birds, elephants, hippos, and crocodiles. As the lake has shrunk, so have the animal populations. Lake Chad is very shallow, only 36 feet (11 m) at its deepest. More than half of it turns into wetlands in the drier seasons.

At its smallest, around 2001, the lake disappeared completely from Niger and Nigeria. Many worry it might vanish completely. However, recently it appears to have reversed course and expanded somewhat. The reasons for the lake's extreme fluctuations are not fully understood. In part, according to the United Nations Environment Programme, they may be the result of overuse by local communities and inefficient management by national authorities. Overgrazing in the surrounding grasslands is causing a decline in vegetation and desertification. Other likely factors are air pollution blowing in from Europe and North America, drought, and climate change in general.

The drying up of the lake has had the most serious impact on Nigeria, where poverty and hunger are fueling terrorism. However, Cameroon reaps an associated misfortune as thousands of refugees fleeing terror in neighboring countries flock to Cameroon, creating a humanitarian crisis in the Lake Chad region.

the northeastern border, the Logone joins the Chari River, which empties into Lake Chad. There are a number of lower plateaus toward the south. The steep falls that occur as some of the rivers flow to the coast have been exploited to produce hydroelectric power.

The western highlands, sometimes called the Cameroon highlands or the grasslands, is an area with volcanic activity, though today the only volcano that is still active is Mount Cameroon, actually the sole major mountain in West Africa. In the highlands, there are numerous volcanic lakes. In 1986, Lake Nyos—a volcanic crater lake—released a noxious gas that was blamed for the deaths of 1,746 people.

The coastal lowlands are characterized by numerous rivers that form swampy areas as they break up into small streams. This terrain provides ideal conditions for mangrove trees, which flourish along parts of the coast.

MOUNT CAMEROON

Fako is the highest point on Mount Cameroon, which is, in turn, the highest point in the country. The mountain is also known by its indigenous name,

Craters formed in the top of Mount Cameroon after the volcanic eruptions in 2000.

Mongo ma Ndemi ("Mountain of Greatness"), or Mont Cameroun in French. Standing at a height of 13,435 feet (4,095 m), it rises 14 miles (23 km) inland from Cameroon's coast on the Gulf of Guinea. The port of Limbé, formerly called Victoria, lies at the southern foot of the mountain. The seaward side of the mountain has the reputation of being one of the wettest parts of Cameroon; more than 394 inches (1,000 centimeters) of rain fall a year. In 1861, the British explorer Sir Richard Francis Burton (1821—1890) was the first European to climb to the top. Still active, volcanic Mount Cameroon last erupted in 2000.

CLIMATE

For an equatorial country, Cameroon has a surprisingly variable climate. This is due to a number of local factors affecting weather patterns, although Cameroon has a largely tropical climate. The main seasons are not summer and winter but wet and dry periods. Around Douala on the coast, the rainy period often lasts eight wet months. This area has over 169 inches (429 cm) of rain a year. In the Lake Chad Basin, on the other hand, the wet season lasts only a couple of months, and annual rainfall there is only 100 inches (254 cm).

Lightning streaks across the sky during a thunderstorm in a rain forest in Cameroon.

Altitude affects the temperature, so there can be sizable differences in average temperatures even within the same area. Coastal regions with an altitude of 2,954 feet (900 m) record average temperatures of 70 degrees Fahrenheit (21 degrees Celsius), whereas the city of Douala, which is at sea level, has an average temperature of 79°F (26°C).

The Harmattan, a dry wind that blows from the Sahara during the dry months, also affects the climate. The wind carries with it sand and dust from the desert, adding to the aridity; thus, the north of the country, which is nearer to the Sahara, has a longer dry season.

This tree in a Cameroonian rain forest has buttress roots—large, thick roots that grow out from the trunk. These roots help support and stabilize the massive tree in the thin soil of the tropical forest.

FORESTS AND GRASSLANDS

The combination of different temperatures and rainfall produces two major types of vegetation in Cameroon: equatorial forest and tropical grassland. Rain forest and mangrove swamps are found near the coast, where rainfall is highest. Mangrove trees anchor themselves in swampy water by means of long, spreading roots that reveal their architecture when the tide is out and their complex root system is exposed on the mudbanks. The hardwood rain forest consists of mahogany, ebony, sapelli (or sapele), iroko, and obeche trees. The obeche, or African whitewood, is a large deciduous forest tree that commonly grows up to 200 feet (61 m). Because of the cash value of the hardwood, the rain forests have been aggressively logged.

Moving inland from the coast, annual rainfall decreases, and the forest thins out. A mix of forest and grassland then gives way to savanna, where trees and bushes are few. Acacia and baobab trees survive here because they can shed their leaves, prolonging their ability to survive dry periods. There are a few hundred species of acacia trees in Cameroon, and one of them, *Acacia catecu*, produces the dye that was the original source of khaki coloring. The large and impressive-looking baobab tree is distinguished by its massive trunk, part of the tree's water-storage system. A rich variety of grasses grows in Cameroon's savanna belt, the tallest of them reaching over 6 feet (2 m) in height. Evergreen trees and papyrus grass thrive along the riverbanks, benefiting from their close proximity to water.

This variety in vegetation, plus regional factors such as the presence of rich volcanic soil around Mount Cameroon and other parts of the western highlands, accounts for the diverse agricultural potential of the country.

FLORA AND FAUNA

Cameroon has a marvelous assortment of flora, including grasses and trees, and fauna. Elephants, crocodiles, rhinoceroses, hippopotamuses, lions, panthers, cheetahs, and gorillas are all found in Cameroon, though their numbers are not significant. Smaller in size but still impressive are tarantulas, also known as palm spiders, which grow as big as saucers. Warthogs—one of the world's endangered animals—still live in the more remote forests. Another rare animal is the drill, a large primate with a short tail, similar to a mandrill. It has a red lower lip, brown fur, and vividly colored buttocks.

The drill, (*Mandrillus leucophaeus*), is a monkey related to baboons and mandrills. One of Africa's most endangered animals, it is found in southern Cameroon.

RESOURCES

Petroleum was discovered in the Gulf of Guinea in the mid-1970s, and crude oil was first produced there in 1977. In 2018 and 2019, Cameroon produced 69,000 barrels per day.

There is tremendous potential for hydroelectric power. Cameroon relies on the existing hydroelectric dams and hydroelectric stations to generate 90 percent of the electricity for its towns and cities.

Limestone and a kind of rock called pozzolana, used in the manufacturing of cement, are found in plentiful supply in Cameroon. The country also benefits from deposits of bauxite, diamonds, and iron ore, but these resources are not yet exploited commercially on a large scale.

This aerial view shows the cityscape of Yaoundé, the capital of Cameroon.

CITIES

The placement and development of many towns in Cameroon can be traced back to the country's colonial era. The first Europeans to arrive at the coast of Cameroon were part of a 1472 Portuguese expedition led by Fernando Po. A tribal settlement already existed on the coast at Douala when the first European traders arrived in this part of West Africa. Later, under German colonial rule, the place developed into the country's largest port.

During their domination (1884—1916), the Germans established a trading station at Yaoundé to lock out their French and British trading rivals. No large villages existed in the Yaoundé area until a fort was built and a telegraph station was established. It then developed into an administrative center for trade, and mission schools were set up. Yaoundé grew to become the country's capital city and remains the administrative and educational center, with a population close to 2.5 million, as of 2019.

Other important cities include Bamenda, Bafoussam, and Nkongsamba, all located in the more densely populated western part of the country. Most towns in Cameroon are growing rapidly, especially in the west, as many people are migrating to the cities from surrounding rural areas. Since most Cameroonians are not wealthy, the increasing numbers of people moving to urban settings is creating shantytowns where the quality of housing is inadequate and basic facilities such as running water, sanitation, and electricity are in short supply.

Limbé, situated on the coast near the southern foot of Mount Cameroon, is Cameroon's second-largest port after Douala. Coffee, cocoa, palm oil, tea, bananas, and rubber are exported through Limbé. Originally christened Victoria, in honor of Queen Victoria of Great Britain, the town was founded in 1858 by Baptist missionaries. Limbé had a population of 84,223 in 2005, the last time a census was taken.

INTERNET LINKS

https://www.britannica.com/place/Cameroon/Land
This encyclopedia provides an overview of Cameroon's geography, climate, soil, and plants and animals.

https://www.climatechangenews.com/2019/05/16/lake-chad-not -shrinking-climate-fuelling-terror-groups-report
This article examines the link between Lake Chad and terrorism.

HISTORY

Sculpted masks such as this one were a feature of secret societies among certain ethnic groups in Cameroon.

2

HUMAN HISTORY IN THE REGION now called Cameroon extends back to about 50,000 BCE—nearly to the dawn of human history itself! The Baka people, an ethnic group once known as Pygmies, were probably the earliest inhabitants of the area, and small groups of the hunter-gatherers still reside in the Cameroonian rain forest today.

Little is known about the deep history of the region. In fact, most histories of Cameroon begin with the arrival of the Europeans.

BEFORE COLONIALISM

The country now called Cameroon was never a unified entity prior to European colonization in the nineteenth century. Rather, it was a fluid patchwork of kingdoms of diverse peoples with their own cultural identity and history. Migration of people between one state and another was common and was usually dictated by shifting patterns of economic relationships.

One of the earliest known kingdoms in Cameroon was formed by the Sao people around 500 CE. It was located on the shores of Lake Chad. In the northwestern grasslands of today's country, kingdoms of Bamum, Bamileke, Nso, and Bafut people existed between the fourteenth and sixteenth centuries.

Early European settlement of the Cameroon region was very limited because of the threat of malaria. Because of that and other deadly illnesses, that part of Africa came to be known as the "white man's grave." By the 1870s, when the anti-malarial drug quinine became available in large quantities, Europeans began to explore and quickly claim the interior regions of western Africa.

Bantu speakers from equatorial Africa are the first people known to have invaded the south and west of the country. In the eighteenth and nineteenth centuries, the Fulani—a pastoral Islamic people of the western Sahel, the semidesert edge of the Sahara—conquered northern Cameroon.

The first Europeans to navigate down the west coast of Africa as far as the Gulf of Guinea were Portuguese explorers in the late fifteenth century.

TRANSATLANTIC SLAVE TRADE

The Portuguese established trading posts and small colonies on the west coast of Africa. These places would later serve as transport hubs for the transatlantic slave trade. The trade began with small numbers of enslaved Africans, but as demand grew on the plantations of the Americas, other European nations—the British, French, Spanish, and Dutch—became involved in the lucrative trade.

By the late eighteenth century, Cameroon and the delta area of the Niger River in Nigeria were the focal points for the embarkation of slaves for the Americas. An estimated twenty thousand men and women left those shores every year, never to return. Douala, a trading post at the mouth of the Wouri River in Cameroon, served as a center for the slave trade. Many of the Douala (or Duala) people themselves, an ethnic group who lived in that region, served as middlemen.

African traders became rich by organizing large slave-hunting expeditions in the interior. The slaves were kidnapped or traded inland and then passed along through a string of middlemen until they reached the coast, where European trading ships waited offshore. The trade developed a shipping network that was later used for the transportation of commercial goods when the slave trade finally ended in the 1860s.

GERMAN COLONIALISM

The closing decades of the nineteenth century witnessed a struggle between European powers for lucrative new colonies in Africa. A growing demand for natural resources in Europe made it profitable for each nation to take

THE SCRAMBLE FOR AFRICA

The nations of Africa are a relatively modern creation. As recently as the nineteenth century, vast regions of the continent's interior remained unmapped and unknown to the outside world. Native peoples lived in various tribal kingdoms with their own rich cultures and traditions. However, to Europe and the rest of the Western world, Africa was "the dark continent." In this case, "dark" meant not only unexplored but also savage, wild, and uncivilized.

Africa's seacoast regions were more accessible and therefore better known to Europeans. Beginning in the fourteenth century, Portugal and other nations set up trading posts, forts, and attempted colonies along coastal areas. North Africa, however, had long been dominated by Muslim cultures and was essentially a barrier to Europe. Until the eighteenth and nineteenth centuries, European powers were more interested in the Americas.

European colonies in the Americas eventually won their independence. At the same time, the Industrial Revolution was radically changing Western economies and ways of life. For these and a variety of other reasons, Europe took another look at Africa.

Ongoing piracy along the Barbary Coast and a trade dispute between France and Algiers sparked the French invasion of Algiers in 1830. By 1875, the French conquest was complete. Meanwhile, European leaders sent explorers into the heart of Africa to map it, convinced that the African people needed the "civilizing" influence of European culture.

Europe therefore began to see Africa as ripe for the taking, and a virtual land grab began. By 1884 and 1885, what has come to be called "the scramble for Africa" was on. A new age of imperialism began in which major Western powers tried to secure and gain supremacy by building an empire of overseas properties. Colonies were a status symbol as well as a source of natural resources, labor, and military recruits.

In 1884, thirteen European countries met in Berlin to draw up the rules of African colonization and literally split the continent among themselves. The colonizing powers were primarily Britain and France, with Germany, Italy, Portugal, Belgium, and Spain taking much of the rest. Lines of new nations were drawn arbitrarily, sometimes cutting apart historically united tribal regions. By 1902, 90 percent of Africa was under European control. By 1914, the European takeover of Africa was complete, with only Ethiopia managing to remain sovereign.

possession of a piece of Africa and treat it as an extension of their own state. This became known as the "scramble for Africa."

The Duala people, living around the Wouri River, signed a treaty in July 1884 that permitted German rule in the area close to the river. Palm oil, rubber, tobacco, tea, coffee, bananas, and cocoa were all valuable products worth exporting, so the Germans eventually expanded their domination inland by setting up convenient routes to their plantations. This enterprise brought the colonists into conflict with local traders, who until then had always traded with Europeans on the coast. Violence broke out whenever the locals resisted German incursions.

Although the period of German colonialism lasted only from 1884 to 1916, it was a very important period because, for the first time, a boundary was established around the region that would evolve into Cameroon. Mission schools were set up by Germans that eventually produced a small elite group of literate clerks, pastors, and teachers. The Germans also changed the name of their new territory on the west coast of Africa to Kamerun. Douala was developed as the main port, and new settlements were built inland.

World War I German officers (*in white*) stand with colonial troops in drill formation at the German Government Station in Kamerun around 1915.

Toward the end of their colonial rule, the Germans started segregating Douala into separate white and black areas, as well as forcibly relocating inhabitants. The German authorities wanted to acquire the land, which was becoming increasingly valuable, without having to pay local landowners the market price. Resistance to the segregation was organized under the leadership of Rudolph Douala Manga Bell, who was later tried for treason and executed. On the day that he died in 1914, another rebel, Martin Paul Samba, also faced a firing squad for offering to help the French if they would remove German rule.

World War I, which broke out in 1914, was partly a struggle between European superpowers to gain control of profitable imperial possessions. Kamerun, a land rich in natural resources, was invaded by French and British armies. When the war ended in 1918 with the defeat of Germany and its allies, Kamerun was divided between the victors. Under a League of Nations mandate, the larger share of the territory, about four-fifths of Kamerun, went to France and became French Cameroon. A smaller area in the west that bordered Nigeria went to Great Britain. The country was thus divided into two parts. The British territory was itself split into British Southern Cameroons (or Southern Cameroon) and British Northern Cameroons (or Northern Cameroon).

A SHARED COUNTRY

The British sector was attached to Nigeria, a larger and more valuable part of the British Empire, and many thousands of Nigerians moved into South Cameroon. In British Cameroon, the English language was used in schools and the administration, whereas French was used in the rest of the country. Neither the French nor British imperial powers were particularly interested in encouraging their nationals to settle in Cameroon. Their main interest was to exploit the land's economic possibilities by developing plantations, especially for coffee.

Meanwhile, Douala was growing in importance as a major port, and a small but significant number of industrial companies were set up in the coastal area, including a hydroelectric plant and an aluminum-processing plant. After World War II, these developments attracted an even greater number of Europeans to Cameroon. Because European migrants were offered the best employment opportunities, racial tensions began to develop. A new movement, the sense of nationalism, began spreading among Cameroonians.

NATIONALISM

The influx of Nigerians into British Cameroon, where many of them held minor positions of authority in the police force and the judiciary, led to the feeling that Cameroon was becoming a subcolony of a colony. This strengthened calls from the indigenous peoples for reunification of the two parts of the country. A labor organization in French Cameroon, Union des Populations du Cameroun (UPC), conducted its activities in secret and called for active resistance to French rule.

In 1956, a form of self-government was introduced by France. The colonial power remained in control of foreign policy, and a coalition government was established. This government fell from power in 1958, and a second coalition government was formed under the leadership of Ahmadou Ahidjo (1924—1989) in 1959. There were now calls for complete independence, and Ahidjo's government offered amnesty to UPC nationalists, who agreed to cease their guerrilla war against the French administration.

INDEPENDENCE FOR FRENCH CAMEROON

French Cameroon gained independence on January 1, 1960, and the Republic of Cameroon came into existence. It was not generally known at the time, but agreements had been made to preserve French economic and military interests to ensure a peaceful transition to independence.

There was no constitution when Ahidjo became ruler of the country in 1960. He consolidated his own political power and tailored a constitution that

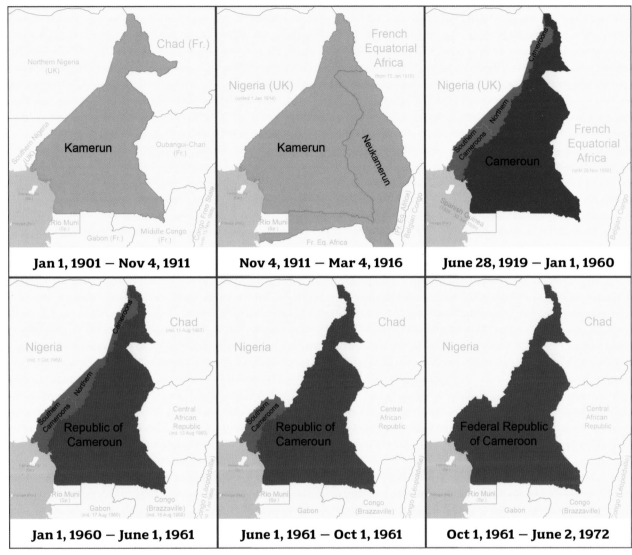

| Jan 1, 1901 — Nov 4, 1911 | Nov 4, 1911 — Mar 4, 1916 | June 28, 1919 — Jan 1, 1960 |
| Jan 1, 1960 — June 1, 1961 | June 1, 1961 — Oct 1, 1961 | Oct 1, 1961 — June 2, 1972 |

suited the interests of the government and the people he represented. New elections took place four months after independence, and although the UPC was allowed to take part, Ahidjo's party, the Union Camerounaise (UC), won fifty-one of the one hundred seats in the parliament. Ahidjo himself ran for election as president and, being the only candidate, was elected. His party sought to avoid open conflict and formed a coalition government with all the parties except the UPC.

This series of maps shows the changing boundaries and names of what would become today's Republic of Cameroon.

COMPLETE INDEPENDENCE

In British Cameroon before 1960, there were appeals for reunification with French Cameroon, but at the same time, there were calls by other groups for a merger with Nigeria. The British rulers gradually allowed greater autonomy to Cameroon representatives in the Nigerian federal government. In 1961, voters were given the choice between unification with Nigeria or with the new Republic of Cameroon. The result for British Southern Cameroon was overwhelmingly in favor of reunification with the former French Cameroon. British Northern Cameroon chose to join Nigeria. In October 1961, the Federal Republic of Cameroon came into existence, uniting the British and French colonial areas into one new country.

THE AHIDJO YEARS

Ahidjo was the first president of the republic and remained the undisputed leader of Cameroon's government until 1982. He was a dictator, personally commanding nearly all aspects of political life. He began by forming a single political party, the Cameroon National Union (CNU), in the French-influenced eastern part of the country and merging it with a number of different parties in the British-influenced west of the country. Parties failing to cooperate with this process were outlawed and their leaders arrested and imprisoned. In theory, it was possible for new political parties to be formed, but in reality it was extremely difficult, and no emerging party was allowed to develop an effective voice. Military force was used to destroy the remnants of the UPC opposition to the new state. Labor unions were forced to form a single organization, which then came under the political control of the government.

State power became centralized in Yaoundé, and previous forms of local government were dismantled. In 1972, the federal system of government was abolished and the country became the United Republic of Cameroon. A number of provinces were created, each one overseen by a governor and regional officers. All government officials were appointed by Ahidjo. Cameroon was under a political, not military, dictatorship because Ahidjo was able to use his great power to win cooperation from individuals and groups who might

otherwise have mounted opposition to his rule. At the same time, it was generally known that political opposition to Ahidjo would not be tolerated, and civil rights such as press freedom were severely constrained.

Ahidjo's ability to single-handedly rule his country was aided by the financial support of the French government and the commercial backing of his regime that came from the powerful business interests that remained largely under French control. At the grassroots level, Ahidjo was able to hand out jobs and contracts to local people who would continue to support him. The civil service went through a process of "Cameroonization," replacing French bureaucrats with Cameroonian ones. This helped to ensure loyalty to the government.

Ahmadou Ahidjo (*center*), the first president of Cameroon, attends ceremonies on January 1, 1960, in Yaoundé to mark the country's independence.

THE BIYA YEARS

Paul Biya, the president of Cameroon, is shown in his younger years.

Ahidjo resigned in 1982, handing over the presidency to his prime minister, Paul Biya (b. 1933). A peaceful and voluntary transfer of power in Africa is not a very frequent event, so it was commonly assumed at the time that Ahidjo did not intend to relinquish all his power. However, Biya emerged as an independent leader who was not willing to act as a puppet for Ahidjo. In 1983, the resignation of Ahidjo as president of the CNU and his replacement by Biya marked a decisive shift of power. A plot against the Biya government was said to have been uncovered, and rumors circulated that Ahidjo was implicated in this.

Once in power, Biya proclaimed the need for a more democratic form of government. Ahidjo, who left the country and went into exile in France in 1983, was found guilty of involvement in a plot to take over the government and was sentenced to death. Although his sentence was later reduced, it provoked another coup attempt in 1984 in which an estimated five hundred to one thousand people were killed by government forces, and many others were detained or imprisoned before the rebellion was crushed. Ahidjo died of natural causes in 1989 in Dakar, Senegal.

Following the coup, Biya obtained 99.98 percent of the votes in a presidential election in which he was the only candidate. By 1986, Biya was still not allowing opposition parties to register, but he changed the name of his own party from UNC to Rassemblement Démocratique du Peuple Camerounais (Democratic Rally of the Cameroonian People, or RDPC), probably to distance himself from Ahidjo. In the 1998 presidential election, Biya was again the only candidate, and with 98.75 percent of the votes he prevailed for a new term in office.

In May 1990, the Social Democratic Front (SDF) was formed without permission from the government. A founding rally was held in Bamenda, but although it was intended to be peaceful, riots broke out and six people were killed. A draft for a multiparty system was laid out by the president, and after a few months, more than twenty parties had registered, every one of them in strong opposition to Biya's ruling party. Biya dismissed the plans for a multiparty system, banned opposition rallies, and placed seven provinces in Cameroon under military rule.

A campaign for civil disobedience was launched in 1991, and a general strike was called. The strike did not end until the government agreed to support the work of a constitutional committee, which had formed to discuss the political future of Cameroon. Legislative elections took place in 1992, and opposition parties were allowed to run. However, Biya did all he could to ensure his reelection, including shutting down all independent newspapers.

In the presidential election of 1992, Biya won 39.9 percent of the votes and the opposition leader, John Fru Ndi, got 35.9 percent. Observers from the United States reported election fraud. A state of emergency was then declared in the western provinces. John Fru Ndi and many others were put under house arrest. In the 1997 legislative elections, the opposition parties called for a boycott of the undemocratic elections, but the opposition was split, and Biya was reelected.

Biya has been reelected in every election since then, most recently in 2018. The next election is to be held in October 2025. It should be noted that Biya will be ninety-two years old at that point, should he decide to run again.

DISRUPTIONS AND CRISES

Although the long years of dictatorship were nobody's idea of true democracy, the strongmen in charge of Cameroon did manage to keep a semblance of peace and stability, for the most part. However, in recent years, several crises have disrupted the country—terrorism, Anglophone separatist agitation, and popular protests against the corrupt Biya government.

Terrorism from neighboring Nigeria has overflowed into Cameroon's northern Lake Chad region. Boko Haram, a jihadist group based in northeastern Nigeria, increasingly launched violent attacks in Cameroon throughout the 2010s. The group, which in 2015 renamed itself the Islamic State in West Africa (but is still commonly known as Boko Haram), seeks to implement an extremely strict form of Islam, called Wahhabism, throughout Africa. It uses kidnapping,

Relatives and officials at Orly Airport in Paris welcome the seven members of the Moulin-Fournier family arriving from Yaoundé on April 20, 2013. The French family was released after being kidnapped and held in Nigeria for two months by Boko Haram.

suicide bombings, and conventional armed attacks against politicians, religious leaders, security forces, and civilians. In 2013 and 2014, the group kidnapped seven French tourists, a French priest, ten Chinese workers, and the wife of Amadou Ali, Cameroon's deputy prime minister. In some—perhaps all—cases, large ransoms were paid to secure their release, but not all details are known. For the most part, though, most kidnappings have been of Cameroonians, including women and children.

In addition to terrorism itself, Cameroon has had to deal with influxes of hundreds of thousands of refugees from neighboring Nigeria and the Central African Republic. The refugees, living either in camps or in Cameroonian towns, add tremendous strain on some of the country's most economically vulnerable regions. Basic resources such as food and shelter, as well as social services such as medical care, are far from sufficient, even for the permanent population.

Meanwhile, on another front, English-speaking Cameroonians—about 20 percent of the population—have grown dissatisfied with being an aggrieved minority group in their own country. Since 2016, some twenty different separatist groups have emerged in Cameroon's North-West and South-West Anglophone regions—bordering English-speaking Nigeria—fighting to establish a separate country they call Ambazonia. What began as a nonviolent protest movement turned into an armed insurgency after President Paul Biya's security forces fired live ammunition from low-flying helicopters into protesting crowds in late 2017. The resulting conflict between the government and the insurgents has come close to a civil war.

INTERNET LINKS

https://www.bbc.com/news/world-africa-13148483
The BBC News timeline of Cameroonian history begins in 1520.

http://thecommonwealth.org/our-member-countries/cameroon/history
A quick overview of Cameroon's history is available on this site.

https://www.washingtonpost.com/graphics/2019/world/cameroon-anglophone-crisis/?utm_term=.05b7de076db2
This article about the growing linguistic conflict in Cameroon includes a video.

GOVERNMENT

The flag of Cameroon waves in the breeze.

3

WHEN CAMEROON BECAME AN independent state in 1960, the people needed to choose a form of government and to write a constitution. A sense of identity to unite all Cameroonians—over and above the many ethnic loyalties that divided the citizens of the new state—had to be created, too. In particular, people from the British and French areas of influence and people from the northern and southern parts of the country had to be pulled together to live in harmony. Without some sense of shared identity, there loomed a fear that the nation would fall apart.

Many newly emerging African states were confronted with such problems in the 1960s. Many of them, such as Cameroon, had been shaped and defined by colonial experiences that had never nurtured national identity. In many cases, including in Cameroon, the physical boundaries of the states had been artificially created by resident colonial powers, and new national territories had forced very different ethnic groups together, each with its own language and culture. Such volatile situations gave new governments excuses to create authoritarian political systems.

In 2019, there were eighty-two women serving in the two houses of the Cameroonian parliament, for a total of 29.3 percent.

Native Cameroonian soldiers stand at attention on January 1, 1960, in Douala, as Cameroon becomes an independent republic.

THE CONSTITUTION

A constitution is a country's fundamental legal document. The history of Cameroon's constitution reflects the changes the country has undergone since achieving independence in 1960.

The constitution of 1961 made Cameroon a federation of two states under a single president. A new constitution was written in 1972 when the United Republic of Cameroon was formed under President Ahmadou Ahidjo. That constitution increased presidential powers and forms the basis for the document that remains in effect today.

In 1984, however, it was revised again under President Paul Biya. This version changed the country's name to the Republic of Cameroon, redrew the lines of the provinces, and changed the line of succession to the presidency.

THE PREAMBLE OF THE CONSTITUTION

We, the people of Cameroon,

Proud of our linguistic and cultural diversity, an enriching feature of our national identity, but profoundly aware of the imperative need to further consolidate our unity, solemnly declare that we constitute one and the same Nation, bound by the same destiny, and assert our firm determination to build the Cameroonian Fatherland on the basis of the ideals of fraternity, justice and progress...

So begins the preamble to the Cameroon Constitution.

Although a preamble, or introduction, is not a necessary part of a constitution, many countries include one in their founding document. A preamble usually establishes the purpose and underlying philosophy of the nation.

The preamble to Cameroon's constitution is the only portion of the document that has remained unchanged since 1960. It establishes lofty goals of equality, freedom, security, and respect for all, regardless of gender, race, religion, or political opinion. It guarantees freedom of expression, assembly, and the press, as well as the right to join trade unions and the right to strike. It promises a fair trial and the assumption of innocence until proven guilty. It absolutely forbids torture or any other "cruel, inhumane or degrading treatment" at the hands of the state. It establishes the state as a secular nation that recognizes the freedom of religion and worship. It also promises to protect the environment and to use Cameroon's natural resources to the benefit of all citizens.

To say that Cameroon's reality has fallen short of such goals is perhaps an understatement. Nevertheless, the constitution exists as an aspirational document that the country can still use as a motivation for achieving the sort of government it truly desires.

In 1996, the constitution was revised again. It remains in effect, with modifications made in 2008. The most recent amendments provide for the president to be immune from prosecution for acts as president and allow him or her to run for unlimited reelections. These revisions sparked public outrage and protest.

STRUCTURE OF GOVERNMENT

Executive powers are in the hands of the president, who is the head of state and chief of the armed forces. He appoints all the ministers. The president is elected for a period of seven years by direct and secret universal suffrage, which is granted to citizens at the age of twenty. There are no term limits. Since 1982, the president has been Paul Biya. The next presidential election is to be held in October 2025.

Cameroon's prime minister, Joseph Dion Ngute, attends the Humanitarian Conference for Nigeria and Lake Chad Region in Oslo, Norway, in 2017.

The prime minister is meant to be the head of government (although their actual power is limited) and is appointed by the president. In 2019, President Biya appointed Joseph Dion Ngute as the prime minister.

Legislative power is held by a bicameral, or two-house, parliament. The Senate consists of one hundred seats, with seventy members indirectly elected by regional councils and thirty appointed by the president. Members serve five-year terms. The next Senate election is scheduled for 2023.

The National Assembly has 180 members, directly elected by simple majorities in multiseat constituencies. They serve five-year terms. The republic is divided into ten administrative regions, each headed by a governor. Each region is divided into departments or divisions. The last Assembly elections were delayed until October 2019. It remains to be seen when the following round will take place.

AHIDJO'S GOVERNMENT

From independence until 1982, Cameroon was governed by Ahmadou Ahidjo. He created a presidential system of government that invested nearly all the powers of state in his own position as the president.

The constitution was altered so the president became the head of state, the most powerful person in the government, and the commander in chief of military

Ahmadou Ahidjo was born in Cameroon in 1924 and died of a heart attack while in exile in France in 1989, after having been sentenced to death for alleged involvement in an antigovernment coup.

He served as president for twenty-two years, from May 1960 to November 1982, and although he insisted on retaining power strictly for himself and his own party, he kept his country free of the internal power struggles that destabilized other African nations that had gained their independence around the same time.

His greatest achievement was overseeing the peaceful and successful emergence of Cameroon as one united nation, formed from two separate and not always harmonious states. A Muslim from northern Cameroon, Ahidjo maintained control and stability with the active support of the French government.

forces. The National Assembly was awarded no executive powers at all and simply rubber-stamped whatever legislation the president proposed. Ministers, governors, and judges were all appointed by the president. When elections for the National Assembly took place, the party that received the majority of votes automatically won all the available seats. This made it virtually impossible for any new party to win representation in the assembly because they would have to obtain over 50 percent of all votes in the country. Thus, the CNU always remained in power.

BIYA'S GOVERNMENT

When Paul Biya gained power in 1982, he announced the need for more democracy and changed the constitution to allow non-CNU members to run in presidential elections. Nonetheless, there was still no opposition when

Biya won his first full term as president in 1984. The concentration of power in the hands of the president remained intact. What changed was the new president's willingness to use his great power to bring about some relaxation of the dictatorial state's practices and his pledge to introduce democratic reforms.

Important changes appeared in the running of government ministries. People were appointed because of their skill and aptitude for the jobs and not just their political usefulness to the president. In 1987, Biya wrote a book entitled *Communal Liberalism* in which he explained the kind of government he wanted to bring about and the need for the "establishment of a new political society." He also made it clear that although a multiparty state was a goal to aim for, it would be necessary to maintain one-party rule for the time being.

Biya proclaimed the need for a National Charter of Freedom, too, a defined set of human rights that would apply to all Cameroonians. However, that ideal seems to be set in words but not in practice under Biya's rule.

In 1984, Biya changed the country's name from United Republic of Cameroon to simply the Republic of Cameroon, asserting that the people had become united, and so there was no longer a need for the word "United." As recent events since 2016 have proved, however, the sense of unity between the Anglophone and Francophone parts of Cameroon has greatly disintegrated.

POLITICAL PARTIES AND OPPOSITION

Cameroon was a one-party state from 1966 and was dominated by the CNU. In March 1985, the CNU became the Democratic Rally of the Cameroonian People, or RDPC. The change of name was not enough to persuade people that the governing party was interested in serious democratic reforms, and the second half of the 1980s witnessed political unrest and violent clashes between government forces and groups demanding political change. In 1990, a constitutional amendment established a multiparty system, although the RDPC remained dominant. Other constitutional reforms in 1993 sought to decentralize the government. The main opposition was the SDF (also known in French as Front Social Démocrate, FSD), which challenged Biya for the presidency.

Since 1990, the SDF has been led by John Fru Ndi (b. 1941), who ran for president against Biya in 1992. He lost but claimed victory in what he called a fraudulent election. He ran again in 2004 and 2011, again unsuccessfully.

In 2008, Fru Ndi called for a national "day of mourning" on April 21 to commemorate the individuals who died during the 2008 anti-government protests and what he called the "death of democracy" in Cameroon. He opposed the changes made to the constitution that year, saying they would allow President Biya to be the lifelong dictator of Cameroon.

Cameroonian political opponent John Fru Ndi gestures during a political meeting in Yaoundé on the eve of the 2011 presidential election.

Despite constitutional declarations to the contrary, corruption is alleged to be endemic in Cameroon. Bribery, nepotism, and cronyism are common in almost all sectors of the Cameroonian government and economy—especially in the judiciary, public services, and customs. The courts are said to be inefficient and extremely vulnerable to political interference. Bribes will often win a favorable judgment—indeed, they may even be required. Although anticorruption laws exist, they are often used to target political opponents. High-level officials act with impunity. Article 66 of Cameroon's constitution, which requires government officials and civil servants to declare their assets and property, is not enforced.

Systemic corruption extends to everyday life. Demands for bribes are commonplace in many situations, from gaining school admission to fixing traffic tickets.

Fru Ndi, who grew up in the English-speaking region of North-West Province, has so far rejected separatism. During the Anglophone Crisis, he has twice been kidnapped—and released—by Ambazonian separatists, who want him to align with their cause.

THE JUDICIARY

Cameroon has a Higher Judicial Council that is constitutionally responsible, together with the president, for guaranteeing the independence of the judiciary and the equality of all citizens before the law. The role of the council is to advise the president on the nomination of magistrates and judges and to monitor the performance of their duties.

The Cameroonian legal system has been shaped and influenced by the dual British-French colonial heritage. It has been described as bijural, consisting of two legal systems, English Common Law and French Civil Law. This makes Cameroon one of the few examples of a dual legal system in the world. French civil law applies in the eight French-speaking regions, and English law applies in the two English-speaking regions. The recent effort to unify the two systems has added to the Anglophone conflict.

The legal system of Cameroon consists of the Supreme Court, two courts of appeal, high courts, and circuit courts. The Supreme Court has the power to decide whether a bill should be taken before the National Assembly when a disagreement between the president and the legislature arises. There is also a court of impeachment that can judge the president in cases of high treason and other government ministers in the event of a coup against the government.

The Palace of Justice in Douala houses one of Cameroon's courts of appeal.

CHIEFS

In precolonial times, the power of government operated through a system of chiefs. Each chief, or *fon* (FON), had his own special hut and, depending on local political arrangements, had a number of more powerful chiefs he was subservient to and lesser chiefs that he could rule. The chief combined the powers of judge and jury for his own village, leading to the view that the chief was an autocratic ruler with dictatorial powers. This was not true, however, in most cases. Many chiefs governed with the input of a council of older and more respected members of the community. This modifying force tempered the chiefs' unilateral powers.

Chiefs today no longer wield any official political power, although it is not uncommon for a chief to hold a local government post. Official or not, the chiefs still exercise significant social influence as pillars of tradition and continuity.

INTERNATIONAL RELATIONS

Cameroon has a long-standing and important relationship with France, since a sizable part of the country used to be a French colony. At the time of independence, France played an important role in shaping the government that emerged in Cameroon, and it still maintains an influence in the land it once controlled. The two countries have economic, diplomatic, military, and cultural links, and together they strengthen and preserve a relationship that was forged in the era of colonialism.

Critics sometimes argue that Cameroon is still too closely tied to its old colonial master. They worry that the economic and military links encourage a relationship of dependency. Nevertheless, Cameroon has developed friendly relations, both economic and diplomatic, with other nations both within and outside of Europe.

Cameroon's historical ties to Great Britain account for its continuing membership in the Commonwealth of Nations.

HUMAN RIGHTS

Cameroon has a mixed record on human rights, and it is trending downward. The Anglophone Crisis and Boko Haram terrorist attacks have both led to a worsening humanitarian situation in the country. Reports of abuses by all sides are growing.

Under the aging President Paul Biya, government security forces have behaved with impunity against civilians. Torture, executions, arrests, and deportations have increased. In 2017, government forces responded to peaceful demonstrations by the Anglophone community with live ammunition shot from low-flying helicopters. At least a dozen demonstrators were killed. In addition, elections appear to be rigged, refugees from neighboring Nigeria have been abused, and international human rights standards have been increasingly ignored.

Meanwhile, corruption is rampant, journalists and human rights activists have been silenced, and same-sex relations remain illegal.

INTERNET LINKS

https://www.amnesty.org/en/countries/africa/cameroon
Amnesty International reviews the human rights situation in Cameroon.

https://www.constituteproject.org/constitution/
Cameroon_2008?lang=en
The Constitute Project provides the 1972 Cameroonian constitution, revised in 2008, in English.

https://www.ganintegrity.com/portal/country-profiles/cameroon
This anti-corruption site provides a look at the problems in Cameroon.

https://www.hrw.org/world-report/2019/country-chapters/
cameroon
The Human Rights Watch report on Cameroon is available on this site.

ECONOMY

An oil platform dominates the view from
the city beach of Limbé, Cameroon.

4

CAMEROON ONCE HAD ONE OF THE strongest economies in sub-Saharan Africa. In general, the countries of sub-Saharan Africa are extremely poor, so Cameroon's economy needs to be understood within that context. Nevertheless, Cameroon began its life as an independent nation in relatively good economic condition and enjoyed stability for many decades. Various factors have since weakened it. However, it's still in better shape than many of its neighbors. Whether that will continue to be the case in light of current separatist unrest, terrorist incursions, and troubling political leadership remains to be seen.

Cameroon, which the World Bank classifies as a lower-middle-income country, has a market economy centered largely on oil. Although oil prices have been falling since the 1990s, oil still accounts for some 40 percent of the country's exports. Cameroon has a wealth of other natural resources as well, including natural gas, timber, minerals, and agricultural products.

Cameroon is building Central Africa's only deep-sea port in the fishing town of Kribi. The ambitious project, financed primarily by China's Export-Import Bank, is due to be completed in 2035. It will include twenty berths for container ships; an oil and gas terminal; a large industrial zone to process timber, cotton, and cocoa; and highways and railways connecting to Cameroon's main cities and mines.

Gross domestic product (GDP) is a measure of a country's total production. The number reflects the total value of goods and services produced over one year. Economists use it to determine whether a country's economy is growing or contracting. Growth is good, while a falling GDP means trouble. Dividing the GDP by the number of people in the country determines the GDP per capita (per person). This number provides an indication of a country's average standard of living—the higher the better.

In 2017, the GDP per capita in Cameroon was $3,700. That figure is very low and ranked Cameroon 182nd out of 228 countries listed by the CIA World Factbook. *For comparison, the United States that year was number 19, with a GDP per capita of $59,500. Cameroon's neighbors Republic of the Congo and Nigeria fared only slightly better, with figures of $6,800 and $5,900, respectively. Chad was lower, at a mere $2,300, and the Central African Republic held the lowest place on the list, number 228, with a GDP per capita of only $700.*

These have helped the economy rebound from the effects of the shrinking oil market. The economy continues to grow.

One of the greatest threats to the economy is the high incidence of corruption in government and business. Such corruption discourages foreign investors, which in turn prevents the government from undertaking large construction and infrastructure projects. This becomes a vicious circle: without adequate infrastructure, such as modern roadways, foreign industries and businesses are reluctant to operate in the country.

Also adding stress to the economy is the mounting civil unrest in the Anglophone regions. Wars are bad for business all around and certainly keep tourists and investors away.

AGRICULTURE

Three out of four Cameroonians live and work on their own land, producing around 90 percent of the country's food. The national economy is heavily dependent on agriculture. In 2017, agriculture contributed 16.7 percent to the

GDP. The average size of a farmstead is small, around 7 acres (3 hectares), but this is adequate to maintain a lifestyle that is reasonably self-sufficient. Cash crops include coffee, bananas, peanuts, palm oil, palm kernels or seeds, cotton, rubber, and cocoa beans from cacao trees.

In the north, farmers primarily grow grain and raise animals. Lake Chad and the rivers flowing into it provide a rich supply of fish. In the south, there is more agricultural variety—millet, rice, bananas, peanuts (which are called groundnuts), corn, and cassava are grown, and cattle, goats, sheep, and horses are raised. On the plateaus farther south, the conditions are suitable for growing cotton, cacao, coffee, and tobacco.

The altitude and climate of the western highlands is ideal for planting coffee, corn, peanuts, bananas, and plantains. The forested areas in the south produce sorghum, sweet potatoes, and yams, as well as more cacao than any

other region. Cameroon is among the world's largest producers of cocoa.

TRADE

Colonial footprints are seen in most aspects of Cameroonian life, and the economy is no exception. When the country gained independence, around 60 percent of its exports went to France. This has gradually dropped to 12.6 percent in recent years. Cameroon has developed trading ties with other countries, especially China, but France is still important.

A man pulls cotton bales in the town of Touboro to prepare them for export.

Cameroon's major exports are crude oil and petroleum products, lumber, cocoa beans, coffee, cotton, tea, rubber, peanuts, bananas, and aluminum. Imports consist mainly of industrial and household goods, motor vehicles, other transportation equipment, spare parts, fertilizers, and pesticides.

FOREST DESTRUCTION

Cameroon produces more cut trees for lumber than any other country in Africa, and this has resulted in very few virgin forests remaining. Even though Cameroon still has one of the largest tropical forests on the continent, this rampant harvesting has depressing consequences for the environment and wildlife of the region. Forestry experts believe that Cameroon is exploiting this resource at a faster rate than it can sustain through replanting, and the long-term result will be the total destruction of a valuable and beautiful resource.

Part of the problem arises from governmental concessions sold to private companies to exploit an area of forest. In addition, the prevalence of corruption is poorly controlled in Cameroon, and this means that the more unscrupulous companies—the ones that pay the biggest bribes—are often more likely to obtain logging contracts. This tends to sideline the environmentally responsible

companies, leaving corrupt ones with opportunities to abuse their position through excessive logging without regard for replanting or conservation.

A commercial company engrossed in maximizing its profits does not look at a forest with the same eyes as a conservation group. Conservationists regard the forest as a whole, seeking to preserve its ecological identity, and they understand that any one area of a forest contains different types of trees growing in harmony.

From a narrow commercial point of view, it makes sense to select and log only the most valuable trees in an area. It has been estimated, however, that 10 percent of a forest area is sacrificed in the process of getting to and removing a single selected high-value tree. In this way, over a period of time, the entire forest will be seriously damaged, even though only relatively few trees will have actually been cut down. Building access roads into previously

Workers load logs from massive trees in a timber yard in southeastern Cameroon.

dense forests encourages illegal hunters to poach because their activities become a lot easier. In addition, antelope, chimpanzees, and gorillas are hunted down and shot for sale as "bushmeat" in the local towns.

TOURISM

Tourism is a relatively minor industry in Cameroon, but with the right development, it could play a much larger role in the economy. Tourists are attracted to African states because of the opportunities to see exotic wildlife and to experience novel and dramatic landscapes.

Cameroon is able to tap into this tourist market because it possesses two important assets. First, Cameroon has an astonishingly rich ecology, ranging from rain forest to rolling savanna—and that includes the most varied flora

A tourist sits by a waterfall in Cameroon.

and fauna in all of Africa. Eight national parks are open to foreign visitors, and because such tours tend to be expensive, they generate high revenue from a relatively small number of visitors. One of the most well-established and successful destinations is Waza National Park, where elephants, antelope, giraffes, lions, and monkeys roam freely.

A second asset is the country's relative economic and political stability, a status that makes tourists feel safer in Cameroon than in some of the neighboring states. As previously stated, however, that stability is increasingly threatened. That said, some 822,000 international arrivals were logged in 2014.

Obstacles to attracting greater numbers of tourists include the poor infrastructure—traveling around the country is difficult. Also, corruption extends down to everyday encounters, and tourists don't like being harassed by police who expect bribes.

Cameroon's flagship airline, Cameroon Airways Corporation—known as Camair-Co—began operations in 2011. It took the place of the previous national airline, Cameroon Airlines, which went bankrupt and ceased flying in 2008. Camair-Co operates out of Douala International Airport, Cameroon's busiest airport. The largest public airport is Yaoundé Nsimalen International Airport, located 16 miles (27 km) south of the capital city.

INTERNET LINKS

https://borgenproject.org/facts-about-poverty-in-cameroon
This aid organization presents ten facts about poverty in Cameroon.

https://www.britannica.com/place/Cameroon/Economy
This online encyclopedia provides an overview of Cameroon's economy.

https://www.heritage.org/index/country/cameroon
The Index of Economic Freedom rates the country's overall business environment.

https://www.worldbank.org/en/country/cameroon/overview
The World Bank provides an up-to-date overview of Cameroon.

ENVIRONMENT

One of the Ekom-Nkam waterfalls cascades down a rocky ledge in Korup National Park in Cameroon's South-West Province. The location was the site of the 1984 film *Greystoke: The Legend of Tarzan, Lord of the Apes.*

5

CAMEROON IS SOMETIMES CALLED "Africa in miniature" because its many ecological zones reflect the diversity of the continent. Only a bit larger than Sweden, the country boasts over eight thousand plant species and a wide range of iconic African animals that includes gorillas, black rhinos, elephants, and cheetahs.

National parks and protected areas of Cameroon cover about 4.4 percent of the country. That is equivalent to about 4.9 million acres (2 million ha). However, even within protected forests, destruction is heavy. In recent decades, more than half of the historic forest cover has been cleared for farms and settlements. Agricultural clearing is the primary cause of deforestation; however, logging—both legal and illegal—has opened up vast tracts of the remaining primary forest. In 2019, Cameroon was reported as being one of ten nations worldwide with the highest percentage of illegal logging.

Additionally, the semiarid northern rangelands are being overgrazed, and the country's coastal mangrove swamps—rich environments for fish and other species—have been exploited, polluted, and otherwise damaged by human activities. Air pollution caused by industrial chemicals and vehicle emissions is a significant environmental problem. Overfishing and poaching threaten the wildlife, and safe drinking water is also a concern. Volcanic activity, flooding, and insect infestations also cause problems.

The Cameroonian rain forests are ancient woodlands. They are lush with diverse plant and animal species, including drills, chimpanzees, forest elephants, gorillas, and leopards. Many animal and plant species exist only in these forests and nowhere else in the world.

A suspension bridge spans a rushing river in the jungle in Korup National Park in Cameroon.

NATIONAL PARKS AND RESERVES

Ten national parks and other protected areas have been developed in Cameroon to provide large safe areas for wildlife and to preserve the flora of the region. Some of them have become popular tourist destinations.

Korup National Park was established in 1986, having first been designated as a forest reserve in 1937. This area is in Cameroon's South-West Province, adjacent to the international boundary with Nigeria. Korup contains the widest variety of tree species in any rain forest in Africa. The area receives a great deal of rainfall and relatively little sunshine, and this, combined with poor accessibility, has allowed the natural rain forest to flourish.

There are twenty-nine villages within the Korup area, six of them inside the park. Because the lives of the local inhabitants are so intricately interwoven

WORLD HERITAGE SITES

Since 1975, the United Nations Educational, Scientific and Cultural Organization (UNESCO) has maintained a list of international landmarks or regions considered to be of "outstanding universal value" to the people of the world. Such sites embody the common natural and cultural heritage of humanity, and therefore deserve particular protection. The organization works with the host country to establish plans for managing and conserving its sites. UNESCO also reports on sites that are in imminent or potential danger of destruction and can offer emergency funds to try to save the property.

The organization is continually assessing new sites for inclusion on the World Heritage list. In order to be selected, a site must meet at least one of ten criteria. These required elements include cultural value—that is, artistic, religious, or historical significance—and natural value, including exceptional beauty, unusual natural phenomena, and scientific importance.

As of 2019, there were 1,092 sites listed, including 845 cultural, 209 natural, and 38 mixed properties in 167 nations. In Cameroon, two natural sites are on the main list. One is the Dja Faunal Reserve, which was added to the list in 1987. The other is the Sangha Trinational, which encompasses three contiguous national parks in the northwestern Congo Basin, where Cameroon, the Central African Republic, and Congo meet. Cameroon also has three UNESCO Biosphere Reserves, which are special natural sites for testing new approaches to interactions between social and ecological systems, including conflict prevention and the management of biodiversity.

with the forest, they have been educated about wildlife and forest care, trained in local technical colleges, taught regional handicrafts, provided with fertile land outside the park for family farming, and employed as park guards. These measures reduce poverty and stop the villagers from hunting animals indiscriminately, possibly killing endangered species. The project has been encouraging because many weapons—previously used by the villagers in hunting—have been handed over to the authorities.

Waza National Park of Cameroon is home to antelope, giraffes, ostriches, gazelles, lions, and elephants, as well as many different birds. It is open to the public for around six months a year, but every vehicle that enters the park must have an official guide. The park is a UNESCO Biosphere Reserve.

A hippopotamus enjoys the waters of the Benue River in Bénoué National Park, Cameroon.

The Bénoué National Park covers an area of 444,790 acres (180,000 ha). The Benue River (also called the Bénoué River), home to large numbers of hippopotamus colonies, flows along the park's eastern border. It also has large numbers of elephants, lions, warthogs, waterbuck antelope, monkeys, and crocodiles. The park is a UNESCO Biosphere Reserve.

Bouba Njida National Park lies in a remote 543,632-acre (220,000 ha) area on the border with Chad. There, antelope, black rhinoceroses, and lions flourish. Dinosaur fossils can also be found in this park. The park was the site of a massive elephant slaughter in 2012, when between 450 and 650 elephants were massacred by poachers. The poachers were reported to be Sudanese and Chadian horsemen armed with Kalashnikovs, who easily overpowered the park's five guards.

Dja Faunal Reserve, covering 1,299,774 acres (526,000 ha), is one of the best protected rain forest areas in Africa and is located in the south-central part of the country. The terrain encompasses evergreen and semi-evergreen forests. Conservation of great apes in this reserve is a prime concern. The park is home to at least fourteen types of primates, including several endangered species, such as the western lowland gorilla, chimpanzee, white-collared mangabey, mandrill, and drill. The reserve shelters more than one hundred species of mammals, including the endangered forest elephant, bongo (a striped antelope), and leopard. Dja Faunal Reserve is a UNESCO World Heritage Site.

Deng Deng National Park was created in 2009 specifically to protect a population of six hundred gorillas and other threatened species such as chimpanzees, forest elephants, buffalo, and bongos. The park spreads over 224 square miles (580 sq km), an area approximately the size of Chicago.

Takamanda National Park was also created in 2009. Takamanda forms part of a transborder protected area with Nigeria's Cross River National Park and has been established especially to protect the world's rarest gorilla, the Cross River gorilla.

Mount Cameroon National Park opened in 2010 with the expectation that it would bring benefits to the local population as well as conserve the environment. Almost sixty traditional chiefs from around the area gathered at its opening ceremonies to sanctify the new venture.

The Cross River gorilla is found only in a few forested regions of Nigeria and Cameroon.

Elephants and chimpanzees roam the park's forests, and many species of rare plants thrive in them. People benefit from the resources found on Mount Cameroon, but the human presence puts the entire ecosystem at risk. Poaching and the steady encroachment of towns have placed the animals at risk of extinction. The urbanization of the area has also meant that the water resources are in jeopardy. Farming and agriculture threaten the ecosystem on Mount Cameroon. Trees and brush are cut down and used as firewood. The soil is very fertile and suited to growing crops, but converting some of the land into an agricultural cooperative has meant that in many places, it is now over-farmed and has lost its natural fertility.

By designating the area as a national park, the government created investment opportunities there, particularly in roads and infrastructure. The park has become an active tourist destination, providing the local jobs necessary to keep the park operational.

DEFORESTATION

Cameroon has one of the highest deforestation rates in Africa, losing hundreds of thousands of acres of forest per year, mostly to logging and agriculture. For example, of the different tree species found in the Mount Cameroon region, *Prunus africana*, or red stinkwood, is the most valuable because of its medicinal properties. Locally, it is used to treat chest pain, malaria, and even mental illness. Its bark contains active biochemicals used in the treatment of prostate gland disorders. Moreover, many trees are dying due to the poor harvesting methods found in large-scale commercialization.

Unsustainable logging practices also lead to deforestation and forest degradation. Present-day logging practices inflict damage to broad areas of forest, as roads must be built to move large machines deep into the woods and to carry the lumber back out. There is flagrant wasting of wood at the logging sites in the forest, and there is still more waste at the sawmills, often located at remote areas that are hard to police.

Contour maps essential in the planning of road construction and bridge alignment are often not available. Topographical maps and maps detailing species in the targeted area of forest to be logged may not exist. Logging can therefore take place in an area where it is too hard to haul the cut logs to a sawmill or where many trees are indiscriminately destroyed in an effort to get to the tree species that an operator wants to harvest.

Population growth is a significant cause of deforestation and forest degradation. Rural-to-urban migration has been increasing. Population growth has kept pace with food production, so the total area under cultivation has increased proportionately. This has been achieved through the slash-and-burn system of farming that involves clearing a plot by chopping down and burning the trees and underbrush, planting crops such as corn, cocoyams (taro), cassava, and other vegetables for a number of years, and then leaving the plot fallow (unseeded) when the productivity of the soil has been exhausted. Land may be left fallow for more than a dozen years. The farmer simply starts the process somewhere else. This is called shifting cultivation.

Deforestation is also caused by poorly defined property rights. Most logging takes place on communal land that is administered by the state on behalf of the local community. The people have the right to produce on the land, but resources such as trees belong to the state. As a result, the people do not have the incentive to manage the land properly. The communities come into conflict with the logging companies when trees—which provide fruit, oils, food, or medicinal materials—are cut down to provide milled wood or are simply damaged in the process.

ENDANGERED WILDLIFE

Due to the fast and furious forest exploitation, over forty species of wildlife, such as the black rhinoceros, gorilla, and elephant, are threatened with extinction. The region is home to several endangered primates, including the Cross River gorilla (*Gorilla gorilla diehli*), a rare endemic subspecies of western gorilla; the mainland drill (*Mandrillus leucophaeus leucophaeus*); and the common chimpanzee (*Pan troglodytes*). In recent years, the importance of these animals has been recognized, and parks have been established especially to protect them and their environment.

A chimpanzee is shown here in Cameroon.

International environmental organizations are active in many parts of Cameroon, working to preserve endangered wildlife and threatened lands. Such organizations as the WWF, the African Wildlife Foundation, and the Rainforest Alliance—along with many others—work to educate communities and work with (or compel) the government to better protect the flora and fauna of the nation.

POLLUTION

Poor countries are particularly vulnerable to pollution. Typically, they don't have the money to monitor pollutants, clean up problem areas, or enforce environmental laws. In Cameroon, urbanization, industrial activities, and the aggressive exploitation of agricultural land have led to an increase in the amounts of the many pollutants that are discharged and could reach river waters and have a damaging impact on fisheries.

WATER POLLUTION Rapid industrialization and urbanization are having a harmful effect on water supplies in the cities. Without government oversight, most industries do not treat their effluents before dumping them into rivers and streams. Toxic, cancer-causing chemicals, such as mercury, lead, and arsenic, flow unchecked into the nation's waterways.

In addition, human wastewater from poorly managed septic collection practices leads to underground water pollution, which contaminates drinking water. Few populated areas have modern sewage systems, although some newly constructed systems exist in Yaoundé, Douala, and a few other cities.

A pile of trash accumulates in an abandoned market area.

Contaminated water contributes to the spread of deadly water-borne diseases. From 2011 to 2014, for example, Cameroon reported 26,621 cases of cholera leading to 1,031 deaths.

More recently, cholera broke out in refugee camps in northern Cameroon, where more than 100,000 Nigerians are living in primitive and unsanitary conditions, having fled Boko Haram violence in their home country.

AIR QUALITY Air pollution, both indoors and outdoors, is a major concern in Cameroon. Indoors, some 90 percent of the people use solid fuels for cooking, which is a hazard that particularly affects women and children. Outdoors, car exhaust, wood burning, garbage burning, the use of millions of diesel electricity generators, and petrochemical plants contribute to poor air quality—especially in urban areas.

PESTICIDES Cacao and coffee plantations use large amounts of pesticides to obtain maximum high-quality yields. These pesticides leach into the nearby waterways, polluting the water and killing fish. Birds may also be affected by ingesting toxic fish. Guidelines are being prepared to establish regulations governing the use of pesticides.

INDUSTRIAL EFFLUENTS Certain industries, such as breweries, food-processing plants, tanneries, and sugar refineries, produce organic waste. Sugar refineries at Nkoteng and Mbandjok discharge sewage straight into the Sanaga River—Cameroon's largest river—without any treatment at all. A tannery and at least three breweries also discharge wastewaters directly into rivers. At Limbé, a paper mill and a palm oil factory discharge directly into the sea. These issues are now being addressed because there is a growing awareness of the long-term detrimental effects of pollution on the environment and wildlife—and ultimately on the quality of life in Cameroon. For example, a dam is planned to be built on the Sanaga River that will provide enough water during the dry season to dilute residual discharges from the large pulp mill at Edéa.

INTERNET LINKS

https://www.aljazeera.com/indepth/opinion/2012/03/201235112432745412.html
This article tells the story of the 2012 elephant slaughter in a Cameroonian national park.

https://www.awf.org/country/cameroon
The African Wildlife Foundation site devotes a section to Cameroon.

http://www.mtcameroonnationalpark.org
The home site for Mount Cameroon National Park includes ecological information along with many photos and maps.

https://whc.unesco.org/en/list/407
The World Heritage listing for the Dja Faunal Reserve is found on this site.

CAMEROONIANS

A Bamileke chief in the village of Fongo-Tongo wears richly patterned traditional clothing.

6

CAMEROON IS ONE OF AFRICA'S MOST culturally diverse countries, with some 250 ethnic groups and languages. This, along with its location, makes it more of a cultural crossroads than most other African nations.

In the north, many inhabitants live in a Muslim culture that has been influenced by the trans-Saharan Arab world. In the south, there is an amalgam of different ethnic groups that is rich and diverse, even by African standards. In Cameroon's western highlands, the two dominant groups are the Bamileke and the Tikar.

WESTERN HIGHLANDERS

The people of the western highlands are also sometimes called "grassfielders." Most are Bamileke, a group that migrated south around the end of the sixteenth century. The Bamileke are thought to be related to the original Bantus, who first lived in the western highlands of Cameroon's West Province before spreading across southern Africa. It was the Bantu who first developed the art of working iron and practicing agriculture on an organized scale. Archaeological findings suggest that around 200 BCE, the Bantu began migrating east and south, over time developing into the major ethnic group in Africa south of the Sahara. The prefix *Ba* in the word Bamileke is itself a Bantu word meaning "the people of."

Traditionally, the Bamileke society was a highly ordered one that ranked people in social classes from the chief at the top, supported by a council of elders, down to slaves. Individual Bamileke still consider themselves to be

Many Cameroonian immigrants live in the United States. Aside from the countless numbers of African Americans who can trace their lineage to the enslaved peoples from the Cameroon region, more recent, voluntary immigrants number between 16,894 and 33,181 people, depending on the source. The largest Cameroonian-American community is in Maryland.

members of a specific *fondom* (chiefdom). Of these, the fondoms of Bafang, Bafoussam, and Bandjoun are the most prominent. Secret societies were a common feature of Bamileke social organizations, and they operate today to some extent, although they are not as powerful as they used to be. The most visible characteristic of the Bamileke people, however, is their domestic architecture—their thatched homes are distinctive evidence of their cultural presence in modern Cameroon.

The Tikar are similar to the Bamileke in their lifestyle and art forms, but they claim a separate development from an original group of Tikar people about three centuries ago. Smaller groups belonging to the larger Tikar group are the Babanki, the Fum, and the Kom. Another of these smaller groups, the Mun, flourished for a short while as an independent kingdom.

A Fulani woman holds her baby in Tchamba, Cameroon.

THE FULANI

The Fulani people are found in most West African states and also in Central Africa and Sudan. Around 1000 CE, they migrated southward from northern Africa and began to settle along the coast of West Africa. A Muslim people, the Fulani were involved in various jihads, or holy wars, that led to increases of their power and influence. In the early nineteenth century, a Fulani Empire was established in northern Nigeria and northern Cameroon. This empire was based on an alliance with the Hausa people. Some intermarriages took place, tightening the knot between the two ethnic groups.

Fulani people live and work as pastoralists, grazing their cattle on the savannas. They also farm and grow crops because this offers some insurance against droughts, which can severely reduce the size and worth of their herds. Their traditional culture attaches a high value to the ownership of cattle: the more animals owned, the higher one's social status in the eyes of the neighbors.

In the rain forests of the Cameroonian south live people who have been hunter-gatherers for thousands of years. The Baka, with an average height of 4.9 feet (1.5 m), are one of several Pygmy people in Central Africa. There are at least a dozen such ethnic groups in the central part of the continent, some of which are unrelated to each other.

Pygmyism, in anthropological terminology, refers to the unusually short stature of an ethnic people. Today, the term "pygmy" is sometimes considered pejorative in everyday usage, though there is no single term to replace it. In general, the people prefer to be identified by their ethnic group. Aside from stature, another unifying characteristic of these people is that they are forest-dwelling hunter-gatherers, living a semi-nomadic lifestyle similar to that of the region's Stone Age peoples. The Baka have an intimate relationship with the forest. It provides them with food and shelter, and their whole culture is defined by the forest environment. In Cameroon, there are estimated to be about thirty thousand Baka people.

MYRIAD GROUPS

Cameroon has so many minority ethnic groups that together they make up a majority of the country's population. Many of them are Bantu-speaking people who over the centuries have migrated toward the coastal areas. They include the Duala, the Bassa, and the Bakoko.

Another Bantu-speaking group is the Bulu. Sometimes referred to as the Boulou, the Bulu are a subdivision of the Fang people who live in Equatorial Guinea and Gabon, as well as in Cameroon. The Bulu, who number about half a million

A Kirdi woman stands with her children.

in Cameroon, live by hunting and farming and have been influenced by American Protestant missionaries.

In the mountain districts of the northwest, there are various non-Muslim groups that are known collectively as the Kirdi. They include the Bata, the Fali, and the Podoko. The term Kirdi, which does not describe any one particular ethnic group, means "people without god" and refers to the fact that they are not Muslims. Thought to have originally come from the east, they gradually retreated farther and farther into the mountains in order to elude more dominant groups such as the Fulani, as well as slave-hunting parties.

Near Lake Chad, the Choa people lead a semi-nomadic life. Of Arabic origin, they live in large straw houses with grass roofs, each with an enclosed bedroom inside the large house. The area outside the bedroom, sheltered under the big grass roof, serves as a storage area, kitchen, and enclosure for small domesticated animals.

SOCIAL DIFFERENCES

There is a north-south split in Cameroon that tends to create differences between people. As in other African states, the source of the division can be traced back to the historical legacy of colonialism. One important factor in the north-south partition is a religious one: the Muslim-dominated north tends to have a different cultural focus from the Christian-dominated south. There are also economic differences because the south, where colonialism had more of an impact, is more advanced in terms of education and economic development. The pace of change in the north is slower.

In northern Cameroon, the ethnic group that historically has been the most important is the Fulani. Tensions between the Fulani and some minority groups have smoldered for many generations. In the south, because the Bamileke form the majority, ethnic differences are not as distinct.

Cameroon also has non-ethnic social divisions that are based on the unequal distribution of wealth in the country. In the larger cities in the south, such as Yaoundé, there are well-educated, sophisticated Cameroonians who lead a lifestyle similar to any other wealthy class of people around the world. The lives of these few people have little in common with the lives of the overwhelming majority of ordinary Cameroonians who are not especially well-to-do.

There also exists a social separation between Anglophone and Francophone Cameroonians. What used to be French Cameroon, in the east of the country, had a colonial experience that was different from that in British Cameroon. Many people living in what once was British Cameroon were reluctant to find themselves in a unified state with the Francophone east of the country. This division is still apparent in the choice people make to speak either French or English. In recent years, this separation has turned hostile as Anglophones, feeling like a marginalized minority, seek to break away from Cameroon and create their own country.

INTERNET LINKS

https://www.britannica.com/place/Cameroon/People
This encyclopedia provides a concise overview of Cameroonian demographics.

https://www.voanews.com/africa/cameroon-pygmies-protest-destruction-forest-resources
This article explains how logging companies are destroying the habitat and resources of the Baka people.

LIFESTYLE

Children run and play in Bafoussam, Cameroon.

7

CAMEROON IS A POOR COUNTRY, AND this is reflected in its inadequate housing, poor education and health-care systems, low life expectancy, and numerous other lifestyle indicators. People living in the northern regions are particularly vulnerable to food insecurity, largely because of inadequate services, government mismanagement, corruption, terrorism, and natural disasters. Violence from invading insurgents in the area causes people to flee their homes, suffering further susceptibility to hunger and illness. In the Anglophone regions of North-West and South-West, the mounting separatist conflict has a similar effect.

Cameroon has a large youth population, with more than 60 percent of the population being under the age of twenty-five. However, life expectancy remains low, at about fifty-nine years, due to the prevalence of HIV and AIDS and an elevated maternal mortality rate—the fifteenth-highest in the world.

HOUSING AND HOMES

In recent years, more and more people are moving from rural areas to Cameroon's cities. The trend toward urbanization has occurred more quickly than the construction of housing to meet the need. In 2018, the

An impoverished section of Douala reveals makeshift housing units common in urban areas.

country's minister of housing reported that the government had completed 2,400 new urban housing units, but that is far from what is needed. More units are planned, but meanwhile, people in need of shelter are left to make their own. In urban centers, the structure of such buildings is simple. Cinder blocks (they are called breeze blocks in Cameroon) form the walls, and sheets of tin make the roofs. Crowded shantytowns and slum areas in cities such as Yaoundé are unpleasant, unsafe places to live. They lack potable water and sanitation facilities and often have little or no electricity.

Outside the cities, villages are often cleaner and neater than an urban compound. In a village, each home will have its own latrine. The latrine is actually just a deep hole with a large, flat, lightweight stone as a cover, and for privacy a small screen made with the fiber of leaves from palm trees is used. A village is often just a cluster of homes standing close to one another. The distinction between a small town and a large village is not always clear, but a large village will often have several different compounds, each one consisting of half a dozen huts with walls made of dried mud bricks and separated by bamboo fences.

The building of a traditional mud hut house, one that does not consist of only cinder blocks and a tin roof, usually starts by placing slender wooden posts into the ground to form the outer walls. A second row of posts is then placed inside the first square to form the inner walls, and the space in between is partially filled with layers of raffia palm laid horizontally at intervals of about a foot and tied to the posts at both ends. This provides a structure for the wall, which is then filled and built up with lumps of mud or dried clay. The corners of the square need more support than can be provided by mud or clay alone, and hard stalks of raffia are inserted to form a sturdy ribbing for the corner joints. Today, bricks or cinder blocks are often used for building the corners of rectangular walls.

The grasslands are home to a variety of plants that provide the raw materials for house building. Nails or wire are not needed, and if rope is required to help secure joints, it can be made from the peeled bark of the baobab tree, the fibers of which are pounded together. Mats are made from stalks of millet, which are bunched tightly in clusters and then woven together in a crisscross pattern.

House building is usually reserved for the end of the dry season, when there is a lull in agricultural work and plenty of dry grass to use as material. The roof of a house is often built separately and may be finished and put aside until it is needed. Half a dozen people will then help to hoist the prefabricated roof into place. The family will usually celebrate the completion of their new home with a party.

In small villages in the countryside, a home is more plainly constructed than a house in town. Banana plants, mango trees, and shrubs are planted in gardens surrounding each hut. In addition to providing color and shade, these plants produce food for the family. In a patch of bare scrubland close to the home, a family's goats are tied with rope, and chickens and ducks forage close to their pens.

The Bamileke people in the country's West and North-West regions have had the same basic design for their homes for centuries. The main room is square, and the average length of a wall is about 15 feet (4.6 m). The thatched roof has a distinct conical shape. The walls of the hut are made from mud and bamboo posts. The skill of building can be seen in the construction of a circular platform that rests securely on the square walls and supports the conical roof. Palm fronds surround the walls of the hut, and bamboo posts or boards at the entrance are carved with decorative motifs.

A WOMAN'S LIFE

A Cameroonian woman's life is often more demanding than a man's because she is expected to carry out a long list of daily chores that includes making

A woman washes dishes outdoors on a sunny day.

Women in Cameroon, as in many parts of West Africa, distinguish themselves by taking meticulous care of their hair. Large markets will often have hairstylists, each specializing in a particular manner of braiding the hair. Methods and styles of braiding vary from one part of the country to another, and sometimes styling is as popular

with men as with women. The braided hair often incorporates an arrangement of beads of varying colors and sizes. These can be threaded into the hair in highly imaginative ways and contribute much to the splendor of many hairdos. Among some Fulani men, it is fashionable to have sections of braided hair encased in thin, hanging metal strips, preferably bronze because it can be polished to produce a bright shine.

trips to the local market for food, as well as pounding corn, yams, or cassava to make *fufu* (PHU-phu), a doughy dumpling that is dipped into stews. Fuel for cooking, apart from charcoal, which is purchased, comes in the form of small sticks of wood gathered from the nearest forest. Equally essential is a daily supply of water, and since very few homes enjoy their own tap-water supply, walking to and from the nearest source of water is another daily duty. Women also have the task of looking after their young children and making clothes for them, using cloth purchased in the market and an old sewing machine passed down by the family.

A man's work responsibilities are restricted to clearing land and getting it ready for a new season's planting of cash crops, which he will then tend. The woman may help him with these chores too, and she may devote six to eight hours a day to agriculture in addition to household work. The money that is earned by a man, usually in the wage-labor sector, is typically kept by the man for his own use, but women decide on the use of income from the sale of milk and milk products.

Different ethnic groups have their own traditions defining the role of women and marriage. Marriage often involves more than simply establishing a bond between families. A common practice among many people is that the bridegroom provides the family of the bride with a valuable dowry. This might take the form of an animal, such as an ox. A man can have more than one wife if he can afford a dowry for each of them.

VIOLENCE AGAINST WOMEN

One problem that pervades Cameroonian society is the high level of violence against women, both within and outside of the family. In a 2011 survey of more than fifteen thousand women across all regions of Cameroon, 68 percent reported having experienced physical or sexual violence perpetrated by their husband or partner in the previous twelve months. Of those, 42 percent of the women said the violence occurred "sometimes," and 26 percent said it happened "often."

Female victims of domestic abuse have little recourse and virtually no legal protection against abusive husbands. Those who try to find justice often find themselves socially shunned, threatened, and sometimes killed. Police are often sympathetic to the man or consider the woman's complaint to be a private matter. Judges—should a case ever get that far—often see domestic violence as an expression of a husband's disciplinary rights over his wife. Women are often blamed for angering the husband.

THE LOCAL MARKET

The local market provides people with the daily necessities of life, such as toothpaste, palm oil, rice, cornstarch, and meat. It can be thought of as the African version of a giant supermarket where shoppers can also purchase T-shirts, imported shirts and jeans, plastic shoes, thermos flasks, sugar, printed fabrics for clothing, cigarettes, beer, cotton, and dried foods.

Market day is a big event in a village or small town, especially for the women who have fruit, vegetables, or dairy products to sell, because this is an opportunity to earn a little personal cash. A woman may walk miles to the market to sell just a bag or two of beans she has grown herself. She will set off at dawn from her compound, hoping to secure a prominent place to display her goods. Women also enjoy the opportunity to talk with others.

A larger commercial trader will have hired—or will own—a small truck overflowing with a variety of products. The next day, he will drive on to another market.

Shoppers mingle at a colorful local market in Batoufam.

TRADITIONAL LIFESTYLES

Northern Cameroon is home to several minorities whose traditional lifestyles are gradually adapting to the mainstream flow of the life of the country.

In the far north, the Kirdi people have a way of life that differs from people living in the grasslands, the plateaus, or the rain forest. The Kirdi are a pastoral clan who build their farms on the sides of mountains, where a system of terracing has evolved over the centuries to make maximum use of all available land. Terrace walls, which follow the natural contours of the land, are carefully maintained by Kirdi farmers to preserve the physical integrity of each small field.

Close to the border shared with Chad, the Musgum people live around the Logone River, and their dome-shaped homes built of clay and grass are unique. The domes are over 30 feet (9 m) high and have a small opening at the very top that is closed only during a period of continuous heavy rainfall. The doorways have an unmistakable keyhole shape: narrow at knee-level and then widening out above the hip level.

In modern times, acquired immune deficiency syndrome (sometimes known as acquired immunodeficiency syndrome), or AIDS, has had a devastating effect on sub-Saharan Africa. AIDS is caused by the contagious human immunodeficiency virus, or HIV. This virus originated as a mutation of the similar simian immunodeficiency virus (SIV) found in chimpanzees and monkeys.

By the 1980s, AIDS had turned into a global epidemic. By 1999, HIV/AIDS had become the leading killer of people in Africa. In 2006, scientists determined that HIV originated in a community of wild chimps in southern Cameroon and was first passed to people hunting those animals in the 1920s. By 2010, AIDS had killed more than fifteen million Africans.

Such an enormous loss of life reversed whatever progress many African countries had made in building independent governance and functioning

Demonstrators in Yaoundé call attention to the devastation of the AIDS epidemic in Cameroon.

economies after the era of European colonialism ended. As the outbreak grew through the 1990s, millions of children were orphaned, or infected with the virus themselves. Huge swaths of the adult working population were wiped out by the epidemic, leaving behind severely weakened communities.

Although the incidence of HIV/AIDS is slowing, it is far from eliminated, particularly in sub-Saharan Africa. Antiretroviral drugs now exist that slow the progression of the virus in the body, but not everyone who needs them receives them. Since 2010, new HIV infections in Cameroon have increased by 5 percent, but AIDS-related deaths have decreased by 13 percent.

In 2016, Cameroon had some 32,000 new HIV infections and 29,000 AIDS-related deaths. There were approximately 560,000 people living with HIV, but of those, only 37 percent were using the antiretroviral therapy. However, 74 percent of pregnant women living with HIV were getting treatment to prevent transmission of HIV to their unborn children. Nevertheless, some 4,000 children were newly infected with HIV due to mother-to-child transmission.

Children sit at bench desks in their elementary school in **Batoufam**.

EDUCATION

In 1999, approximately 81 percent of Cameroonian men aged fifteen or over were estimated to be literate, compared with about 69 percent of adult women in the country. This was a marked improvement over conditions in 1995, when the figures were approximately 75 percent and 52 percent, respectively. The latest figures available, from 2015, estimate that 81.2 percent of males are literate, compared to 68.9 percent of females. The numbers appear to indicate that no real progress in literacy has been made over the past twenty years. On a related note, statistics show that boys typically receive two more years of schooling than girls.

When a child reaches the age of around eleven, he or she takes the Common Entrance Test. The result of this test largely determines what kind of secondary school the child can attend. There is no age limit for taking the Common Entrance Test. If the results are good, most students and their parents will choose a government school, mainly because government schools do not charge any fees. The second choice for students—mostly those who have unsatisfactory test results—will be a mission school, but these school fees can be too steep for some families. The third choice is usually a private school, but again there are fees to pay, and the academic standards vary greatly from one school to another. Some private remedial schools cater to students who fail the Common Entrance Test and wish to improve their standards for another try.

Around the age of sixteen, pupils take tests run by two examination boards, one based on the British system and the other based on the French system. Students may choose which language to take the examinations in, though the choice is usually determined by the type and location of the secondary school they attend. There are eight public universities in Cameroon, the most prominent being the University of Yaoundé, and numerous private institutions.

According to the Global Partnership for Education, an international nonprofit organization, the major challenges facing education in Cameroon are "poor quality, weak governance and accountability across the system leading to the inequitable and inefficient distribution of resources, and persistent disparities related to gender, region of residence and income."

STAYING IN TOUCH

Cameroon's old landline telephone system is woefully unreliable, old, and outdated. Very few people use it. However, cellular phones have become quite popular, as the mobile broadband sector has developed rapidly. In 2017, there was a subscriber base of seventy-nine users per one hundred inhabitants; no doubt the figures are even higher today.

PUBLIC TRANSPORTATION

Private transportation is commonly used for commercial purposes such as transporting goods and delivering supplies. Apart from a small elite group in the large cities, few Cameroonians own their own means of transportation.

This does not mean they don't travel regularly; quite the contrary, there's an extensive and inexpensive system of public transportation of cars, minibuses, and small trucks. All of them together are popularly called the bush taxi.

Every village and town has its own designated area where bush taxis wait for passengers. There are few scheduled services, other than between the few large cities, and a bush taxi is ready to depart once the seats are filled with passengers and their luggage is secured on the roof rack overhead. Bush taxis travel to remote villages—life for most Cameroonians would be unimaginable without them.

Roads in Cameroon are, for the most part, unpaved. Of the approximately 48,220 miles (77,600 km) of roads, only about 3,190 miles (5,130 km) are paved.

INTERNET LINKS

https://www.avert.org/hiv-and-aids-west-and-central-africa -overview
This organization provides a comprehensive overview of HIV/AIDS in Cameroon and the surrounding area.

https://www.equaltimes.org/women-and-children-bear-the -brunt?lang=en#.XROJaehKjcs
This article explains how Cameroon's women and children are suffering during the Anglophone conflict.

https://www.foretiafoundation.org/a-situational-analysis-of -gender-based-violence-in-cameroon
This article examines violence against women in Cameroon.

https://www.globalpartnership.org/country/cameroon
Recommendations for improving Cameroon's educational system are spelled out on this aid site.

RELIGION

Paul Bi, a member of the indigenous Bagyeli Pygmy community in the Kribi region, poses with a tool he uses to communicate with the spirits.

8

THE GREAT MAJORITY OF
Cameroonians—about 70 percent—
are Christian, with about 38 percent
of the population being Roman Catholics,
26 percent being Protestants, and the
rest being Jehovah's Witnesses or some
other Christian denomination. About
21 percent of the population is Muslim,
and some 6 percent practice a traditional
African religion. The rest belong to
another religion or have none at all.

That said, the statistics don't tell the whole story because there is a fair amount of overlap between the traditional African religions and the established Christian or Muslim faiths.

TRADITIONAL RELIGION

Traditional religion is a general name for the great variety of indigenous beliefs of African societies. These are not religions in the institutional sense of Christianity and Islam, and there are no sets of dogma nor a holy text, such as the Bible or the Quran. They are animist beliefs, centered on the unifying idea that nature is invested with spiritual forces and that there is a need to coexist peacefully with these unseen powers.

There is a shared sense of continuity between the living and the dead, especially the recently dead, and a belief that communication between the two worlds is sometimes possible. That explains why in some parts of Cameroon the deceased are buried inside the family home. Some Kirdi groups have soul jars stored in the vicinity of their homes so that the dead spirits will have their own homes. A soul jar is similar to a small family shrine, and remembrance offerings are made on special occasions. The shrine of an ancestor will often contain an item once owned by the ancestor.

Ancestor worship is an important aspect of traditional religion. Recently deceased kin are seen as living beings who continue to watch over their family and their village. Thus, people take care not to do anything that might offend these powerful "living dead."

Animist traditions often include magical interventions in cases of illness or personal problems. Even Christian or Muslim Cameroonians may look to traditional practitioners for such assistance. Many people wear amulets or charms as precautionary measures against malevolent spirits.

DIVINERS

In African tradition, a diviner is an intermediary between the physical and the spiritual worlds. Diviners are recognized and accepted by the community as possessing special skills that allow them to discover, or divine, supernatural aspects of life. The attributes that diviners possess are a combination of intuitive knowledge and acquired skills built up over a lifetime of living and working in the community. The diviner's magical and supernatural powers manifest themselves in various ways.

In western Cameroon, for example, spider divination is practiced using earth spiders, or sometimes the land crab, both of which live in underground burrows. A spider diviner will have a small shrine of his own around the entrance to one of these burrows. When a villager seeks advice, the diviner will place special cards, inscribed with symbolic markings, inside the burrow. The cards, known as leaf cards because they are made from the leaves of a plum tree, are arranged around some freshly captured insects or some edible fresh green leaves that are used as bait. In the process of eating the bait, the spider alters the arrangement of the leaf cards, and it is the new configuration of the cards that the diviner interprets for its message.

Although benign indigenous sorcery is legal, the practice of witchcraft is not. Witchcraft in Cameroon is defined as any act of magic or divination intended to harm another person or property, and it is widespread in Cameroon despite its illegal status. For one thing, it's difficult to prosecute a charge of witchcraft because most accusations are simply personal testimonies. Such charges can be made out of malice, and the laws defining witchcraft are vague. For another, witchcraft is a natural outgrowth of traditional beliefs and a deeply rooted cultural norm, particularly in rural tribal communities. However, it's not only the country folk who adhere to these beliefs—high-level political elites are known to participate in the occult as well.

A Bamileke witch doctor is shown here.

In recent years, witchcraft has been aimed at Boko Haram, the terrorist group spilling across the border from Nigeria. The insurgents have launched suicide bombings, kidnappings, and other violent aggressions, particularly in the northern parts of Cameroon. Curiously, in 2015, President Paul Biya encouraged Cameroonians to use witchcraft, despite its unlawfulness, against the group. Although the advice was enthusiastically received by many citizens—and practitioners—analysts saw it as a sign that the president had little confidence in his military to deter the aggressions.

Some soldiers fighting the terrorists believe that wearing a magic object will protect them. They believe bullets will then have no effect on their bodies and will simply fall to the ground "like small pebbles," according to one militia member.

A crab diviner interprets the meaning of a crab's movements in the village of Rhumsiki, Cameroon.

Another traditional means of obtaining a reading is to use a crab shell that is filled with wet sand inscribed with symbols and pierced with small sticks. This mixture is poured over a river crab, and after a period of time while the crab moves around, the diviner interprets the new pattern of the mixture. The new arrangement of sticks and the scrambling of the symbols are interpreted as a communication from a spirit.

CHRISTIANITY

A church service in a Cameroonian Christian church is likely to be filled with music and songs that rely on traditional African rhythms. This willingness of Christian churches to adapt their practices to harmonize with indigenous religions accounts for the successful spread of Christianity across Cameroon and Africa as a whole in the twentieth century.

Most Cameroonian Christians are Roman Catholic. They accept the pope in Rome as the ultimate spiritual leader. With about one-third of Cameroonians among the faithful, the Catholic Church is one of the country's strongest institutions. It operates a network of schools and hospitals and has the ear of the government as well. Meanwhile, Protestants include Presbyterians, Baptists, and Lutherans.

The distribution of Christians and Muslims follows a geographical split, with more Muslims in the north, while most Christians are found in the south of the country. The English-speaking parts of Cameroon are mostly Protestant. This fact adds a religious element to the recent Anglophone separatist crisis in the country, as churches are increasingly targeted in the violence.

A modern cathedral shines against a blue sky in Yaoundé.

MISSIONARIES

Christianity was first introduced to Cameroon in the nineteenth century. An early attempt was the arrival of the Baptist Missionary Society of London in 1844. In 1858, land was purchased from the Bimbia chiefs, and the first religious settlement, a Baptist church, was built there. Baptist missionaries also founded the town of Victoria, now called Limbé. Under German colonial rule, Catholic and Presbyterian groups arrived from Germany and the United States, and bitter conflicts were ignited between the different missions. Missionaries were not allowed, however, to operate at all in Muslim areas.

Missionaries were initially very intolerant of the beliefs and practices of indigenous African religions. Newly converted Africans were forbidden to dance to their traditional village music because it was associated with pagan celebrations. People being indoctrinated into the Christian faith came to feel ashamed of their own cultures and were induced to leave them behind. The attitude of missionaries has changed a lot since then, and their stark intolerance has been replaced by acceptance of many aspects of the traditional belief systems.

BLACK CHURCHES

Until the 1960s, the majority of churches remained securely under the control of whites. As congregations grew, so did the need to recruit and train local people as instructors and clergy. The advent of an African dimension to Christianity was warmly welcomed. Today, this is revealed in the tremendous popularity and spread of independent churches that have adapted their chosen Christian religion to go well with African traditions.

The roles of ancestor worship, polygamy, and traditional medicine were areas of belief that earlier missionaries did not accept, but the new independent churches are more willing to try to integrate these beliefs into their own dogmas. Traditional medicine, for instance, overlaps with the notion of faith healing that is fairly common in some evangelical churches. Moreover, some churches accept, or turn a blind eye to, the practice of polygamy.

ISLAM

Islam originated in the seventh century CE among the Arab people in Saudi Arabia. It rapidly spread north and west, reaching Tunisia by 670 CE and advancing across North Africa and into Spain and Portugal. Most of North Africa fell to Muslim rule, and trans-Saharan trade carried the religion to West Africa, as Arab merchants traveled across the caravan routes of the desert to trade salt for West African gold. What is now northern Nigeria developed important trading centers, and in this way, Islam found its way to Cameroon.

Islam, which means "submission to God," is defined by belief in one god, Allah. Muhammad, who was born in Mecca in Saudi Arabia around 570 CE, is understood to be the prophet of Allah. Muhammad received revelations from Allah and wrote them down. These form the basis of the Quran, the Islamic holy book. Muslims believe that Muhammad is the last and most important in a line of twenty-eight prophets who received instruction from Allah over time. Jesus Christ was one of these prophets, along with Abraham, David, and Moses of the Bible.

Muslims are bound to follow the five pillars of Islam. These are professing one's faith to Allah, praying five times a day, fasting during the holy month of Ramadan, donating a share of one's wealth to the poor, and making a pilgrimage to Mecca at least once during one's lifetime.

Ramadan is the most important month of the Muslim year. Its date changes from one year to the next because it is determined by the lunar calendar. During the month of Ramadan, Muslims have to fast, which means they are not allowed to eat or drink between sunrise and sunset. A joyous three-day festival, Eid al-Fitr, celebrates the end of Ramadan.

Muslims perform the Eid al-Adha (Feast of Sacrifice) prayer in Yagoua, Cameroon, on August 21, 2018.

INTERNET LINKS

https://africanarguments.org/2015/09/08/cameroons-rising-religious-tensions
This article examines the radical form of Islam being brought into Cameroon by outside groups, particularly Boko Haram, and the resulting effect on religious tolerance in the country.

https://www.crisisgroup.org/africa/central-africa/cameroon/b138 -cameroons-anglophone-crisis-how-catholic-church-can-promote -dialogue
The role of the Catholic Church in Cameroon's Anglophone Crisis is part of this in-depth look at the history of the Catholic Church in politics and conflicts in the country.

https://www.globalsecurity.org/military/world/africa/cm-religion.htm
This site provides a good overview of religion in Cameroon, including the use of witchcraft.

LANGUAGE

Men in Yaoundé read election headlines at a newsstand.

9

LANGUAGE IS A POWERFUL FORCE IN uniting—or dividing—people. Because of Cameroon's history of domination by European powers, both French and English are colonial languages that took root in the culture. Also, because the country was once two different colonies, one French and one British, those languages still define each region as either Francophone (French-speaking) or Anglophone (English-speaking). The language divide is further amplified by the country's position in Africa, wedged between English-speaking Nigeria on one side and French-speaking Chad, the Central African Republic, the Republic of the Congo, and Gabon on the other.

French greatly dominates the country and the government. Because of this, the English speakers complain of discrimination and marginalization. In 2017, separatists in the Anglophone provinces began calling for independence from Cameroon. They want to establish their own English-speaking nation, which they call Ambazonia. As the struggle

Ethnologue, an authoritative resource on world languages, lists 283 individual languages in Cameroon. Of these, 274 are living and 9 are extinct. Of the living languages, 270 are indigenous and 4 are non-indigenous. Twelve are institutional, or used in the professions; 98 are developing, or increasing in usage; 70 are vigorous; 76 are in trouble; and 18 are dying.

A French-language
sign in Garoua
in northeastern
Cameroon reads
"End of Wildlife
Passage Zone;
Djaba Agricultural
Zone."

against government forces has grown violent, the situation has come to be called the Anglophone Crisis, or the Ambazonia War.

Although both French and English are Cameroon's official languages, the country has a wide linguistic diversity of twenty-four major African language groups, from at least 250 different ethnic groups. People living within a few miles of each other may speak different dialects of the same language, which explains why places and people often have more than one name. The Fulani, for example, are also known as the Fula, the Fulanke, the Fulbe, the Fellata, and the Peulh.

FRENCH AND ENGLISH

French is by far the more common of the two official languages, used by about 83 percent of the population. English is seldom heard except in the large cities and the Anglophone regions of North-West and South-West. This

is because French Cameroon was a far larger state than British Cameroon. Pidgin English, a version of spoken English, is used mainly in Anglophone areas and less commonly in Francophone regions. Standard English is rarely used, as it is reserved for formal occasions and tends to be spoken only by the highly educated.

Because there is no single language used by everyone, switching from one language to another is common. Linguists call this practice "code-switching." In the course of one day, Cameroonians may need to use up to six different languages. For example, they may speak in English in the former British Cameroon, switch to French when talking to someone from the former French Cameroon, and converse with market vendors and their family members using the local dialects.

Increasingly, however, a combination of French, English, and pidgin English is becoming a sort of shorthand lingua franca, or common language among people who otherwise speak different languages.

English speaking Muslim children attend class at an Anglo-Arab school in Buea in southwestern Cameroon.

Most of the African languages spoken in Cameroon are tonal languages, which means the tone of the voice actually changes the meaning of a word. This linguistic characteristic spills over to the pronunciation of English and is heard especially in pidgin English.

FRANANGLAIS

With nearly 280 indigenous languages, plus French and English as official languages, it can be tricky to choose the right vocabulary to convey a message. Cameroonian youths spontaneously deviate from linguistic rules with the objective of being able to communicate easily, and the resulting lingo has become known as Frananglais, or Camfranglais. It is a mixture of French, English, and Cameroonian Pidgin English. *Je veux go* is a mixture of French and English and means "I want to go" or "I'm leaving." A child might say, "*Tout le monde hate me, wey I no know*," which means "Everybody hates me, I don't know why." Frananglais is not an official language, and its use has been discouraged in schools across the country because teachers say it has a corrosive influence on correctly spoken and written English and French.

CAMEROONIAN PIDGIN

Most English speakers in Cameroon actually speak a version of pidgin English called Kamtok (Cameroon talk). Many Cameroonian children grow up bilingual, learning both their traditional African language and Kamtok. Linguists define a pidgin as a grammatically simplified form of a language, much like a creole.

Far from being a form of "bad English," however, it is a recognized form of communication. Pidgin English has been spoken in Cameroon for about three hundred years, and it is sometimes mistakenly thought of as a very simplified form of English. This may help explain its origins, but it does not do justice to the complexity of Pidgin English, which can be regarded as a language in its own right, with its own grammar and vocabulary.

Common verbs, such as "have" or "did," are frequently omitted, and the letter *s* is often left off the end of a word. *No tok dat bad people* contains the

Saying hello to someone is sometimes not a simple matter of uttering one or two words. Like all languages, African ones can be finely tuned to suit the occasion. When two people meet, the relationship and situation may require more than the word "hello." Sometimes, even if the intention is merely to briefly greet one another then say farewell, an outside observer might guess they are having a long and meaningful conversation. It would be seen as rude to simply exchange only a few words and then go their separate ways.

pidgin word *tok* for "talk" and *dat* for "that;" the sentence translates as "Don't talk to those bad people."

A young man may start a conversation with a woman by asking her where she is going: "*E! Ma sista, usai you di go?*" He may suggest a visit to the local town: "*Make we shake skin for ville.*" The word *ville* comes from French, whereas *shake skin* is pidgin for "to get going" or "to move."

If someone is asking a companion whether he had a good night's sleep, he may ask, "*You sleep fine?*" or "*Day don clean*?" The word *don*, a familiar pidgin expression derived from "done," is often used in a variety of situations to express the idea of something completed. For example the sentence *I don chop fine* means "I've eaten well." A fine chop means "a hearty meal."

Even within pidgin English, there are variations in sentence structure (syntax), grammar, and vocabulary. Some linguists use the term "educated pidgin" to describe one type of pidgin English. For example someone may say, "My friend is my friend," which means that the person is a close and trusted friend.

Linguists have compiled pidgin English dictionaries, but the origins of many words and even whole expressions are not always known or understood. For instance, it is common to refer to a good friend as *my combe* (kom-BAY), but it is unknown whether the word *combe* is derived from the English word "comrade" or whether it originates from a local language. What is known is that pidgin English is a highly developed and creative language that cannot be picked up by a native English speaker in a couple of days. Proficient speakers of pidgin English, when traveling across the country, often find new words and expressions that have evolved solely in one area. Furthermore, due to a constant process of mixing and borrowing, similar to any living language, pidgin English is always changing.

BANTU SPEAKERS

The first Bantu speakers in Africa lived in northern Cameroon for hundreds of years and then, sometime around the first century CE, began to move south. This migration had momentous consequences in terms of language. The relocation took place gradually over centuries, and as Bantu groups split off from the main population movement and settled down elsewhere, various Bantu dialects developed. By the year 1500, most of the central, eastern, and southern parts of Africa were inhabited by Bantu speakers. Their descendants later migrated south from the Adamawa Plateau toward the coast. There is no one language called Bantu. Rather, it is a language family, with about three hundred Bantu languages and dialects now being spoken across Africa.

DUALA AND FULFULDE

Duala (also called Diwala and other names) is the most widely spoken language in the Cameroonian city of Douala. This Bantu language is used by about

Under German rule, Douala was known as Kamerunstadt ("Cameroon City").

87,700 people in the greater Douala region near the coast, and is written in the Latin script.

The language of the Fulani is Fulfulde (also called Fula and numerous other names). It is a member of the Niger-Congo group of West African languages. There are more than one million speakers across all nations, mainly in Cameroon. It is written in Arabic script.

Fulfulde is strikingly different from English. The plural of a Fulfulde word is formed by changing the first consonant and the word ending, whereas in English a change to the end of a word is usually sufficient to indicate a plural. In Fulfulde, a plural often looks and sounds like a completely different word.

INTERNET LINKS

https://www.bbc.com/pidgin
BBC News provides world news in Pidgin English.

https://www.hawaii.edu/satocenter/langnet/definitions/cameroon.html
A comprehensive overview of Cameroonian Pidgin (Kamtok) is given on this site.

https://www.omniglot.com/language/articles/originsofpidgin.htm
Omniglot provides an explanation of how Pidgin English evolved.

https://www.omniglot.com/writing/adamaua.htm
The language of Adamaua Fulfulde is introduced on this site.

https://www.omniglot.com/writing/duala.php
The Duala language is introduced on this site.

https://www.washingtonpost.com/graphics/2019/world/cameroon-anglophone-crisis/?utm_term=.da3d4841f37d
"Divided by Language" is an article on the Anglophone Crisis, and this site includes a video, a map, and many links.

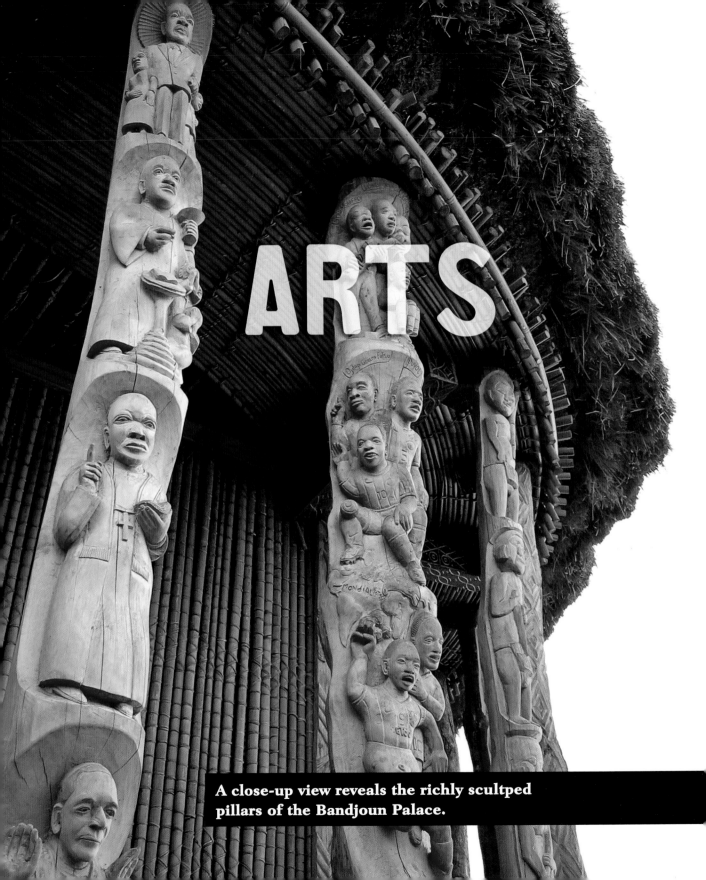

ARTS

A close-up view reveals the richly scultped
pillars of the Bandjoun Palace.

10

CAMEROON IS RICH IN ARTS AND crafts largely because of the variety of cultural groups that make up the country. The grasslands region, comprised of numerous, small, Bantu-speaking societies, is particularly noted for its wooden masks. In the same area, the Kirdi people are very well known for their pottery, and the Tikar are famous for their elaborately decorated brass pipes.

Traditional art is an expression of indigenous religious rites and mysteries. When exhibited in museums overseas, many Cameroonian works are not seen within the context they were created for, and therefore these items are not fully appreciated. Carved human figures were usually produced for a special purpose. For example, some were kept near the entrance of a home to guard the place while the family was out working, and small figurines of pregnant women were held during fertility dances.

GRASSLANDS ART

The grasslands of western Cameroon are home to the Bamileke and Tikar peoples. Their art includes carved masks and figures made from wood and ivory. Popular subjects are human heads, often shown with wide, gaping mouths, and animals such as elephants, crocodiles, snakes, panthers, and tortoises. The spider, an important participant in divination, is one

A masked and costumed performer acts in a ceremony in Babungo, Cameroon.

of the most commonly seen motifs. Detailed figures are carved into lavishly decorated house posts of traditional homes, standing on either side of the entrance. Common domestic items, such as beds and bedposts, bowls, and drinking horns, are also carved with great skill. Chiefs possess intricately carved thrones and stools.

In traditional Bamileke culture, only the chief and a few other high-ranking individuals are permitted to wear an elephant mask during ceremonies or festivities. The elephant, acclaimed as one of the mighty animals of the land, is a symbol of the status and wealth of local chiefs and kings. In some clan legends, the chief has the magical power to turn himself into an elephant. Worn with the mask is an elaborate costume, decorated to draw attention to the high rank of the wearer, and glass beads, which date back to the days of the slave trade, when they were used as a form of currency.

THE BEAUTY OF BEADS

A distinctive art form in Cameroon is the use of beads to decorate wooden sculptures. In past centuries, beads were valuable because they were not easily available and came only by way of trade with Nigeria. Beads, such as pierced cowrie shells, also became a form of currency, and possession of them signified high social status. For this reason, the wearing of exquisite bead jewelry and the use of objects decorated with beads were restricted to royal families. Examples of beaded throne stools include a sacred seat used for royal occasions that has been preserved from the precolonial era. Other beaded items include calabashes (gourds), bottles, and pipe stems. No longer limited to royals, bead necklaces are now popular with present-day Cameroonian women.

In the twentieth century, the art of bead embroidery was developed by self-employed artisans hoping to sell their work to tourists and other travelers. While the original craftspeople were employed only by royalty, it is now common for such work to be carried out by groups of village women working in cooperatives. The range of objects that are embroidered with beads is basically the same as it was in the past: bowls, calabash containers, and stools, as well as figures of lizards and birds. Clothing and jewelry, such as bracelets and even beaded shoes, are also seen nowadays.

The raw materials—cloth, thread, and beads—are purchased by a cooperative from a local market, whereas the wooden sculpture or the calabash that serves as a base is commissioned directly from a local wood-carver. The first stage involves cutting the cloth to match exactly the sculptured shape and then attaching the cloth to the shape. The threaded beads are then sewn onto the cloth. The artisan makes sure that there is no space between the individual beads or the rows of beads. The designs are produced from memory or improvised while working. It takes two days to embroider a small object, one week to finish a bird, and three months or more to complete a large calabash. The work is time-consuming because it is all done without the use of any machines. Moreover, extreme care must be taken to integrate the decorative motif—a spider or a lizard, for example—into the pattern. Women in cooperatives usually work on bead embroidery after the harvest, when they have time to spare.

A potter shows his skill at a handicraft workshop in Bamessing.

POTTERY

Pottery serves many functions in Cameroon. Special pots are made for ritual occasions, celebrating different stages of the life cycle. For example, the birth of twins merits a unique style of pot with two openings at the top.

Some of the most valuable Cameroonian art is pottery crafted solely for the benefit of the local chiefs. These pots are decorated with traditional motifs of animal figures, often represented in whimsical poses such as playfully dancing lizards. Areas where such pottery was traditionally made are now producing high-quality pottery for export to Europe and the United States.

Beautiful pots are also made for ordinary household use. These clay pots are sold throughout the country. In western Cameroon, there is a tradition of making *mimbo* (MEEM-boh) pots, which have extra-large rims to prevent the water or wine inside from spilling. The exteriors of these pots are decorated with sculptures of animals.

TOBACCO PIPES

Tobacco was introduced to Africa in the sixteenth century, and pipe smoking became popular with men and women. The design of a pipe depended on the social status of the smoker, and many of the exquisite examples of carved pipes from Cameroon that are seen in museums around the world were made for chiefs. Their elaborately carved pipes served a ritual purpose and were smoked during fertility festivals. Carved from a variety of materials—clay, metal, gourds, and stone—some of the pipes had skillfully crafted designs decorating the stem and the pot, which holds tobacco or hemp.

Western Cameroon was particularly noted for its clay pipes, and many of the finest examples of pipes were made there. Only men manufactured them, and there were rules about what patterns could be inscribed on the pipes. An ordinary person could not afford to have more than a geometric pattern carved on his or her pipe, but a wealthier patron might commission an animal to be carved. Only the chief had the honor of owning a pipe carved with human and animal figures.

ROYAL ARCHITECTURE

Bamileke culture is distinguished by its traditionally styled village huts. Some of the royal huts, built in the past for their chiefs, survive to this day. One of the best-preserved examples of royal architecture is the impressive Bandjoun Palace, located near the town of Bafoussam. It is a large circular compound, over 50 feet (15 m) in circumference, with a second circle of 20-foot-tall (6 m) carved wooden poles built up outside the first circle. These poles support the single thatched roof of the reception hall that would have been used as a court and for assemblies. There are huts for the chief and separate huts for each of the chief's wives, all with elaborately decorated doorways. The paths in the

palace complex all lead to the village square, which serves as a public area for personal appearances by the fon and as the weekly marketplace.

The Bandjoun Palace is an example of traditional royal architecture in Cameroon.

MUSIC AND DANCE

Cameroon has an exuberant cultural tradition in music and dance. Many of the different ethnic groups have developed their own distinctive styles of dancing and accompanying music that are an integral part of Cameroonian festivals, ceremonies, social gatherings, and storytelling. Traditional dances are elegantly choreographed, though the musical accompaniment may be as simple as stamping feet and clapping hands.

Traditional instruments include bells worn by dancers, clappers, whistles, drums, talking drums, flutes, rattles, scrapers, horns, stringed instruments, and xylophones. The combination varies with each ethnic group and region—and each event. In the south, the xylophone and the drum are featured in nearly every band. In the north, Hausa music from Nigeria, characterized by a

Manu Dibango, (b. 1933), is Cameroon's most famous and influential musician. He is now an international star and the best-known Cameroonian musician outside his own country. In 1983, his receptiveness to new musical styles was showcased when he recorded a single called "Abele Dance," which fused African rhythms with those of New York's hip-hop sounds. He went on to produce his own album, Electric Africa, *which continued to explore ways of joining contemporary electronic music with traditional African rhythms.*

Dibango, born in the coastal town of Douala, first went to France in 1949 to further his studies. He became a saxophonist and pianist and was influenced by the African music coming from the Democratic Republic of the Congo (formerly Zaire). In 1963, he returned to Cameroon. After a couple of

Manu Dibango performs in Paris in 2018.

years, he was back in Europe. When he returned to Douala in 1971, he took the country by storm with his hit "Soul Makossa." This song also became a big hit in the United States and turned Dibango into an international star.

Manu Dibango has pushed forward the frontiers of African music by opening up its traditional rhythms to modernist musical trends from Europe and North America. In his own words, he wants "to let people know that there is an electric Africa also; that people there are dealing with electricity and with computers. Our music isn't going to be only in museums any more. Because Africa is in the Third World, maybe people are thinking that African musicians aren't able to play pianos, synths, or saxes. They want to see Africans beating tom-toms and talking drums. But things are changing."

highly percussive sound and loud drumming, is popular.

Cameroon's musical heritage is at its richest in the south because the port towns there play host to a grand variety of influences from African and Western countries. A result of this fusion was *asiko* (A-see-ko) music, which brought together traditional instruments, such as the xylophone, with Western instruments, such as the acoustic guitar.

What really swept the country, though, was *makossa* music. Championed by Manu Dibango, makossa's enormous popularity lasted through all of the 1970s and 1980s. Although much of the impetus behind Cameroonian music comes from male bands, female musicians have also made their mark. In the early 1980s, Bebe Manga became one of the most successful singers in Africa, and her enchanting songs were hits in French-influenced parts of the West Indies.

A music and dance group from Dschang University performs on the campus in the West Province. The school provides higher education in forestry and agriculture.

NOVELISTS

Most Cameroonian novelists write in French, although their work is often translated into English. Mongo Beti (1932—2001) was one of the foremost writers of Africa's independence generation. In his early works, such as *Poor Christ of Bomba* (1956) and *King Lazarus* (1958), Beti exposes the injustices of colonialism and the racist attitudes it fosters. His novel *Perpetua and the Habit of Unhappiness* (1974) is recognized as an indictment of the way his country was governed under President Ahmadou Ahidjo.

Beti settled in France before Cameroon achieved independence in 1960; he returned to his native country in the early 1990s. In 1978, Beti launched *Peuples Noirs/Peuples Africains* ("Black Peoples/African Peoples"), a political and cultural bimonthly periodical devoted to the defeat of neocolonialism in Africa. Most of his books were originally banned in his native country.

"A FLASH OF SUNLIGHT"

Patrice Nganang (b. 1970) is a Cameroonian writer, poet, and scholar who lives and teaches in the United States. Born in Yaoundé, he is a professor of comparative literature at Stony Brook University in New York. He has won numerous international awards and is especially well known for his 2001 novel Dog Days. *His most recent novel is* When the Plums Are Ripe *(2019). In a statement about his writing, posted on his website, Nganang says, "There is no beauty in despair, but the ability of the human spirit to transcend a history of domination is a flash of sunlight."*

In December 2017, Nganang was taken into custody at the Douala airport the day after publishing an article criticizing President Paul Biya's government for its heavy-handed response to protests by English-speaking Cameroonians. The writer was detained for three weeks before being released and deported back to the United States, where he holds a dual citizenship.

Novelists and other artists are dissuaded from any examination of contemporary political ills, and censorship largely ensures that such issues do not appear in print. Beti got around this problem in his later novels by not setting the stories in Cameroon but creating characters and situations that reflected Cameroonian society.

Ferdinand Oyono (1929—2010) was one of the most renowned anticolonialist novelists of Africa. As a child, he was a choirboy in the Catholic Church, and he studied with a priest. After earning his diploma, he worked as a servant for missionaries and then studied at a high school in France before finishing his education at French universities, writing his first novels at that time. He wrote three novels in his twenties: *Un Vie de Boy* (1956, published in English as *Houseboy*), *Le Vieux Nègre et La Médaille* (1956, published in English as *The Old Man and the Medal*), and *Chemin d'Europe* (1960, published in English as *The Road to Europe*). These novels continue to merit wide readership and favorable critical interest. His novels are representative of the period in which he wrote since they focus on the injustices of the colonial system.

Imbolo Mbue is a Cameroonian-American writer, born in Limbé, Cameroon. After arriving in the United States in her twenties, she earned a degree from Rutgers University and a master's degree from Columbia University in New York. In 2016, she published her first novel, *Behold the Dreamers*, which follows the story of a young Cameroonian family trying to start a new life in New York. The book became a best seller, won several prestigious awards, and was named a "Best Book of the Year" by many reviewers.

INTERNET LINKS

http://www.crafthistory.com/Beads/Cameroon.htm
Examples of Cameroonian beadwork are shown on this crafts site.

https://www.musicinafrica.net/magazine/traditional-music-cameroon
This article argues for authentic traditional music in Cameroon.

https://nganang.com
Patrice Nganang's website includes recent essays and news of his arrest in Cameroon.

https://worldmusiccentral.org/world-music-resources/musician-biographies/cameroonian-music
This world music site has profiles of several popular Cameroonian musicians.

LEISURE

A boy with the flag of Cameroon painted on his face clutches a soccer ball.

MUSIC, DANCE, AND ENJOYING THE company of friends and family are defining features in Cameroonian leisure. Sociability, as much a general African characteristic as it is Cameroonian, lies at the heart of countless festivals and in the way people spend their leisure time.

The country is not immune to electronic forms of entertainment: in the cities, digital video games are popular. Such imported kinds of entertainment, however, have not overturned the appeal of traditional African games such as mancala, a family of board games.

SOCCER

Football (soccer) is very popular in Cameroon, and interest in the sport is growing due to the successes of the national team. Cameroon has qualified for the FIFA World Cup seven times—in 1982, 1990, 1994, 1998, 2002, 2010, and 2014—more than any other African nation. The team, called the Indomitable Lions, qualified for the quarterfinals in the 1990 World Cup, losing to England in extra time. In 1984, 1988, 2000, and 2002, they won the Africa Cup of Nations, and in 2000, they took home the gold medal at the Summer Olympics held in Sydney, Australia.

One of the members of the team that won that Olympic gold was Samuel Eto'o (b. 1981). Before his retirement in 2014, he was Cameroon's all-time leading scorer, and he was proclaimed African Player of the Year four times, in 2003, 2004, 2005, and 2010. More recently, Clinton N'Jie

11

Cameroon has participated in the Summer Olympic Games regularly since 1964, but only once in the Winter Olympics. At the 2002 Salt Lake City Olympic Games, Cameroon's one athlete, Isaac Menyoli, competed in men's cross-country skiing. He fared poorly, but his goal was never to medal. Rather, he wanted to bring media attention to the ongoing prevalence of AIDS in his country.

(b. 1993) has been the Cameroonian footballer to watch. He has been favorably compared to the nation's all-time soccer hero, Eto'o.

Cameroon's women athletes impress as well. Françoise Mbango Etone (b. 1976) became the first female Cameroonian to win a gold medal when she won the women's triple jump at the 2004 Olympic Games in Athens. She won another gold at the 2008 Games in Beijing. At the 2012 Olympics in London, Cameroon's female athletes outnumbered its male athletes for the first time because of the participation of its women's football team. That same year, Cameroonian Annabelle Ali (b. 1985), a freestyle wrestler, was the nation's flag bearer at the opening ceremony.

A RACE UP MOUNT CAMEROON

An annual event in February that attracts many international sportsmen is known as the Mount Cameroon Race of Hope. This marathon involves a race from the Molyko Sports Complex in Buea to the top of Mount Cameroon, an active volcano. The course spans a total distance of 26 miles (42 km). In 2009, the cash prize was $10,000. The starting lineup in 2010 included over seven hundred runners. Thousands of spectators typically come to watch the athletes complete the race. In 2019, Eric Mbatcha won with a time of 4 hours, 45 minutes. It was his third time winning, after having done so in 2011 and 2014. In the women's category, Tata Carine won the race in 5 hours, 35 minutes.

STORYTELLING

A fable is a story with a moral lesson. Most African fables revolve around animals. The telling of fables has been part of African culture for untold centuries, and it continues to this day. Adults and children love to gather in a common village compound to listen to a fable, and storytelling is a shared leisure experience that the entire community enjoys.

The pleasure that people gain from these fables and their function within African societies can be best understood when the significance of certain animals is taken into account. The French anthropologist Claude Lévi-Strauss wrote that particular animals are used because they represent important

FABLES FROM CAMEROON

A Fulani Fable About Rewards *In the middle of the night, when mostly everyone was asleep, a man looking at the sky through his telescope spotted a cow hanging from the moon by a long rope. The cow looked healthy and was mooing loudly, so the man called his friend who was a hunter. Carefully aiming his arrow at the hanging rope, the hunter cut through it. The cow fell to earth and landed in a river. Before the hunter could get to the cow, a fisherman caught it by the horns with his fishing line and dragged it to shore, but the cow quickly ran off, attracted by the sound of mooing from a nearby field. The cow joined other cows in the field, and that evening, the farmer who owned the field stood admiring the new addition to his herd, thinking how lucky he was. This story suggests that those who do the work don't always get the reward!*

A Douala Fable About Two Cats *A man was becoming increasingly worried because his chickens had been disappearing mysteriously from his henhouse every night. He suspected the thief was his own cat, but the cat protested her innocence. The man decided to set a trap. He used one of his chickens as bait and built a clever trapdoor that would snap closed and confine the thief. The next morning, much to his surprise, he found a bush cat—an African wildcat—inside the trap. From then on, no more of his chickens disappeared. So be careful about accusing someone unless you have some evidence.*

A Douala Fable About Strength *The wind liked to blow hard and show off to everyone: "I'm so powerful, I can blow all day and all night and at anyone I like. No one is stronger than I." But a small swallow took up his challenge and told him, "Blow as hard as you wish. Birds can still fly." The wind laughed aloud and challenged all the birds to try to resist his power. The hawk was the first to try, but the wind turned into a mighty storm. In the end, the struggling hawk gave up. Next, the eagle tried. Although it could fly very fast, it could not keep up against the wind. Eventually it gave up. The third bird was a heron. It managed to resist the strong wind for only a very short time and quickly broke a wing trying. The last bird to take up the wind's challenge was the swallow. Being small, it could dive and dart around and successfully resist the wind. This tale teaches you that strength and skill is not a matter of size and that boasting gets you nowhere.*

values. Lions, for example, symbolize courage. Some of the animals used in tales may have become extinct, but that does not lessen their significance in a story because the animals are seen as humans in disguise.

MANCALA

Mancala is regarded as one of the earliest two-player strategy games in the world. Widely popular across most parts of Africa, it is a family of board games, and *warri* (WAR-ree), also called *awele* (a-wee-LEE), is the Cameroonian version of the game. It uses a board with two rows of six scooped-out holes or cups. The objective of the game is to capture the playing pieces or markers, which are seeds, pebbles, or anything else suitable in size, that rest in your opponent's holes in the board. At either end of the board, there is a small cup that collects the captured markers for each player. Although the rules are simple, the subtleties of playing are what make the game so fascinating.

MUSIC

Playing musical instruments, listening to music, and dancing are essential elements in Cameroonian leisure activities. People do not simply purchase recordings of their favorite singers or groups and listen to them in the privacy of their homes, as in the West. Playing music and dancing together in West Africa is a form of popular public culture, one that people participate in as a group. There is a healthy urban musical tradition in Cameroon, but outside of the cities, there are very few professional musicians.

Nearly every community has the resources to produce music to brighten up a social gathering or a special event. The xylophone is one of the most popular instruments and can be easily made using a frame of bamboo placed over dried gourds that act as resonators for the sounds. Drums are not expensive to make and turn up in most village events where music is called for. There are also some specialized instruments that are not commonly found elsewhere. Women play the *oding* (oh-DING), a flutelike instrument that produces light, airy music.

DANCING

Social events everywhere are enlivened by dancing, and urban Cameroon has its own fast-paced dance style called *makossa*. This dance dates back to the 1970s, when mission schools used school bands as part of school life; for instance, music accompanied the stream of students in and out of daily assemblies.

During the planting season, a group of women—as many as twenty or more—will often gather for a drink after a hard day's work in the fields. The village square is a common meeting place for such informal parties, and local beer is passed around in large gourds. Often there is impromptu dancing and singing, with clapping from passersby gathered in a circle around the performers.

INTERNET LINKS

https://www.espn.com/soccer/team/_/id/656/cameroon
This sports site reports news of Cameroon's soccer teams.

https://www.topendsports.com/world/countries/cameroon.htm
This site provides a quick overview of sports in Cameroon, with links to major events.

http://vannier.info/jeux/awele/android/en/awele_rules.html
This games site provides instructions for the mancala-style game of *awele*.

FESTIVALS

In Bafoussam, Cameroon, a Bamileke man performs in a traditional mask and costume at the Nyang Nyang dance festival. The Bamileke festival is one of Africa's oldest carnivals.

MOST PUBLIC HOLIDAYS IN
Cameroon are religious
observances for either the Catholic
or Muslim faith. These are typically
days when government offices, other
institutions, and many businesses are
closed, and many people get the day
off from work or school. They include
Good Friday, Easter Sunday, Ascension
Day, Assumption, and Christmas Day
for Catholics and other Christians,
and Eid al-Fitr, Eid al-Adha, and the
Prophet's birthday for Muslims.

In addition, the secular observances of New Year's Day (January 1)
and Labor Day (May 1) are celebrated, along with Youth Day (February 11)
and National Day (May 20). National Day commemorates the unification
of the English- and French-speaking portions of the country in 1972.

Cameroonians also celebrate a wide variety of local festivals, reflecting
the various traditions of the country. Major stages in the life cycle, such
as birth, puberty, marriage, and death, are celebrated, as are important
agricultural events. Yam festivals, for example, take place in parts of
southern Cameroon when the important food staple roots are ready
for harvesting.

12

Culture Week takes
place in August or
September. During
this festival, young
people travel back
to their villages
to pay respect to
their families and
ancestors. While
they are in their
hometown, the
youth participate
in music concerts,
wrestling matches,
other sports, and
traditional dances
involving sacred
masks.

FESTIVE OCCASIONS

The death of a clan chief and the initiation of a new one may be only a local event, but it will be observed in a major way. In western Cameroon, there is a traditional April festival where the tribal chief disappears into a cave, only to reappear later, as if reborn in the spring, when a ritual procession makes its way to the mouth of the cave. The village diviner marks the foreheads of participants with a mixture of camwood and water, and women are blessed for their continued fertility.

Another joyous celebration is the completion of the harvest around the month of February. Ritualistic harvest festivals are held to ensure the ongoing fertility of crops and women. In the past, a goat would be slaughtered and roasted. Different communities have their own customary practices to celebrate important moments in the agricultural year. Some farmers place a special pot with an opening at the back in their fields, in which small gifts are offered as tribute to the god of the particular field. Before harvest time, there are many festivals that involve children dressing up with face masks and dancing in a field to keep animals and birds out of the plots where they might eat the ripe seeds from the crop in damaging amounts.

FUNERALS

Sad events such as the death of a relative or a friend are still considered festive occasions. They provide the occasion for the most important ceremonies among the forest foraging groups (Baka, Kola, and Medzan).

On the morning of a funeral is the burial, which is a formal event and a show of respect for the relatives of the deceased. The afternoon may be devoted to a community affair that includes the family of the deceased. Family members will gather, each person bringing a supply of palm wine that is mixed together in one large mimbo pot. Participants then drink from this communal stock as a way of affirming their oneness, both in honor of the deceased and in acknowledgment that life goes on.

In traditional African religion, which influences and even underlies Christian dogma on the African continent, there is a close affinity between the recently

For centuries, the grassland areas of Cameroon were divided into a lush mosaic of small kingdoms, with each king having his territory administered by a number of fons, or chiefs. No longer a formal part of governmental structure, chiefs nevertheless continue to play important roles in many rural communities. This is shown by the glamour that characterizes the initiation of a new chief.

Special ceremonies, laid down by ancient custom, are organized and strictly followed. For example, Lake Oku has long been considered sacred. When a new chief was crowned, or enstooled, he was solemnly bathed in the lake's water.

An enstoolment, which comes from the symbolic importance of a specially carved seat on which only the king can sit, is a major occasion, marked by large feasts, dramatic dances using traditional clan dress and masks, and a band performance to provide music for the joyful dances that follow.

dead and the living. A funeral is not regarded as the terminal point of one's life, and this helps explain the festive air that characterizes the afternoon's activities. If the deceased person had a relative or friend who is in a dance society, the funeral will be enlivened by their performance. An elaborate funeral celebration can last up to three days, and the dancing often goes on throughout the night. Approximately a year later, lavish death services honor the deceased, who has then become an ancestor.

REGIONAL FESTIVALS

NGONDO FESTIVAL   This ten-day festival of the coastal Sawa people takes place in Douala at the end of November. Revolving around the spiritual importance of water, the tradition was banned in 1981 because of its secretive rituals, but was revived in 1991. The religious aspect includes communication between the water deities and the Sawa people. A sacred vase is immersed in the Wouri River by an initiate, who dives under the water for about an hour. Magically, he surfaces completely dry with a message from the spirits to foretell the coming year.

People jam onto small boats to celebrate the Ngondo Festival.

Other festivities include arts and crafts exhibitions, traditional wrestling, dance processions, a Miss Ngondo beauty pageant, and dugout canoe races.

FANTASIA   This annual traditional celebration takes place in northern Cameroon. It can also be celebrated anytime to mark a special occasion, such as a visit to the village by an important person. Hundreds of horses often take part, and they and their riders are all attired in bright and colorful costumes. The whole event is a communal celebration and a prime occasion for music and dance.

LELA FESTIVAL   This festival is celebrated annually by the Bali people of western Cameroon. Lasting four days, the festival is held in December. Similar to all local festivals, the Lela festival is an important event for all members of the community, and Bali people who live and work away from home will make a special effort to return home to join in the festivities. It is a time for families to be reunited and old friends to renew loyalties. The village chief is the focus of attention all during the festival. On the first day, he rides on horseback to the local river, followed by all the villagers. A chicken is then sacrificed and examined by diviners. All being well, the diviners will confirm that the spirits are pleased, and the parties can begin. The following days are filled with dancing, feasts, and the firing of guns in celebration. Everyone wears their very best clothes.

NGUON FESTIVAL   Celebrated every two years in Foumban by the Bamum people, the Nguon festival dates back more than six hundred years. The festivities take place over seven days in November, with activities including ritual ceremonies, traditional dances, and food fests showcasing the richness of the Bamum culture.

During the Nguon festival, the Bamum people gather to express their ideas and grievances. The pinnacle of the festivities occurs when the king is deposed, judged on his governance and achievements for the last two years, and eventually reinstated.

INTERNET LINKS

https://afrolegends.com/2014/12/03/the-nguon-festival-a-bamun -tradition-dating-back-centuries
This site tells the story of the Nguon festival.

https://www.timeanddate.com/holidays/cameroon
This calendar site provides up-to-date information about holidays and observances in Cameroon.

FOOD

A woman sells bananas at a street market in Douala.

13

CAMEROON'S CUISINE REFLECTS ITS geography, history, and diversity of ethnic traditions. Food choices vary from region to region. Fish and shrimp are featured mainly on the coast. Beef and poultry are considered delicacies for those who can afford them. Vegetables are plentiful everywhere and are usually accompanied by a spicy sauce. More generally, the Cameroonian diet is characterized by starchy foods as staples.

Many Cameroonians in rural areas of the country grow or hunt most of their own food. There are regional differences in the variety of foods because changes in climate affect the kinds of crops and vegetables that can be grown. In the south, where rainfall is regular, cassava, plantains, yams, and other root vegetables are staples in daily meals. In the north, the temperature and rainfall are more suitable for the cultivation of corn, sorghum, and millet. Throughout the country, palm oil is commonly used, and the groundnut, or peanut, is a favorite ingredient.

HISTORY OF CAMEROONIAN FOOD

Many staples of the modern Cameroonian diet first came with the European explorers of the Americas. They would often sail down the coast of Africa before crossing the Atlantic, or they would return to Africa

The name "Cameroon" is based on the Portuguese word for prawns, or shrimp. In the fifteenth century, Portuguese explorers noted the abundance of shrimp in the estuaries of the Wouri River region and dubbed the land Rio dos Camarões, or "River of Shrimp." Cameroon is the only country in the world named after a crustacean.

CousCous-mais MENU DU JOUR
-MANIOC
TAPIOCA   NDOLE
COKI-PLANTAIN-PATATE   LEGUME.PISTACHE
CONDRE+SAUCE JAUNE   (TOUS LES SAMEDIS)
RIZ PLANTAIN-IGNAME   ROTIS: VIANDE
FRITS DE POMME et PLANTAIN   OMELETTE-POULET
                ROGNON
                POISSON
AUTRES. BOULETTES VIANDE NBONGO CHOBI-MACHOIRON
POULET CONDIMENTS   BOUILLON: PATTE+QUEUE
MARARA-SERUIETTE DE BOEUF D.G/COMMANDE

A restaurant in Maroua advertises its menu of traditional African and Cameroonian dishes in French.

on the way back. The Portuguese brought in such staples as corn, cassava, and tomatoes. Other Europeans soon settled on the Cameroonian coast, and their influence is reflected in the foods eaten today. For example, the French introduced omelets and French bread, and the English started the concept of desserts. For the most part, though, Cameroonians continue to prepare and enjoy their own traditional foods, based on what is available naturally.

Foreign restaurants are found in the larger towns and cities. Douala has Greek, Lebanese, Italian, German, Japanese, and Chinese restaurants, a number of Parisian-style cafés, and small eateries offering pizza and hamburgers. Yaoundé, the capital city, offers a variety of cuisines, including Chinese, French, Italian, and Russian, as well as Cameroonian. In the smaller cities, street vendors and restaurants serve more traditional foods than foreign-inspired dishes.

VEGETABLES

CASSAVA   is shaped like a carrot, with a brown skin and white flesh. The large tubers are boiled and then pounded into a white paste or dried as flour. Sometimes cassava is mixed with other vegetables and meat to make a stew. The leaves of the plant are also eaten, often in zesty sauces.

YAMS   are easy to grow if there is sufficient rainfall. Yams are a basic food in many people's diets across all of Africa. The tubers are pounded like cassava and eaten in a variety of ways. (In the West, the tubers called yams are usually sweet potatoes, a different plant.)

COCOYAMS   are prepared and eaten in much the same way as yams. They are tastier than yams and not as bland. Cocoyams, also called taro, grow vigorously in areas of heavy rainfall, such as the tropical rain forest region of Cameroon.

OKRA   is commonly used in soups and stews because the pods have a thickening effect when cooked. Another name for this vegetable is gumbo.

GREENS   include bitter leaf (*Veronica amygdalina*), a nutritious green used in many dishes. It's the base for *ndole*, or *ndoleh* (en-DOHL-eh), a dish of greens, ground peanuts, and meat or fish, served with shrimp and plantains. Ndole is often called the national dish of Cameroon.

Potatoes and other root vegetables are for sale at a small market.

GRAINS

SORGHUM   is a family of valuable cornlike grasses that can withstand periods of drought. Sorghum grows up to 13 feet (4 m) tall. The lighter-colored sorghum grasses are eaten, whereas the darker ones are fermented to make beer.

- *Only the right hand is used for eating.*

- *If* fufu *is served, one breaks off a piece before dipping it into the soup or stew.*

- *Visitors will be offered food first, but guests must be sure not to eat more than one's fair share of what is on the table.*

- *In traditional homes, men eat first, then women, and then children.*

- *If a bowl of water is passed around after the meal, it is for rinsing one's fingers.*

MILLET is a name given to a group of grain grasses that produce small seeds. They thrive in poor soil and are able to survive drought and intense heat. Millet is used to make porridge, as well as beer, and is pale yellow in color.

CORN is commonly known in Cameroon as maize. Unlike other grains, which came from Asia, corn originated in Central and South America. When the grain is pounded and treated with lime, it produces cornstarch, called corn flour. The young heads of the plant provide sweet corn. Cornmeal, coarsely pounded without additives, is used in various dishes, such as boiled porridge.

MEALS

A typical Cameroonian breakfast consists of a lightly fermented cornmeal porridge with bread and tea. A meal at lunchtime may have rice with fried plantains or a large omelet, and an evening meal could be boiled yams served with fish or meat, or cooked yams mashed with eggs and eaten with fresh vegetables. Beef, chicken, and liver are popular choices when a family can afford to buy meat. Venison, which is more expensive compared with other meats, tends to be eaten only by well-to-do people or at meals marking special occasions. Monkeys, dogs, and cats are sometimes hunted for their meat. Chicken mixed with peanuts and stewed with peppers and onions is a popular family dish.

The most common meal consists of *fufu*, a dumpling-like dough made from pounded corn, cassava, or yams, and *njama-njama*. Njama-njama is a green stew of huckleberry leaves, tomatoes, and onions flavored with hot peppers. After pounding, the fufu is usually boiled until it becomes doughlike and is then placed in an enamel serving dish. The diners have individual plates or bowls of njama-njama. Small amounts of the fufu are taken by hand from the communal dish and dipped in the bowl of njama-njama. Main meals are most often eaten with boiled rice, yams, or plantains. Flavor is added to many dishes by seasoning with local spices and herbs.

Special dishes are reserved for important occasions. Among the Bali people, *shu-a* (SHOO-r) is made with a mixture of pounded peanuts and flour, which is then fried. During a wedding feast, the paste is stirred with water to prepare a drink for the bridegroom and bride.

Chai-khana (CHAI-kah-nah) is a teahouse, usually set up in a taxi stand or bus station. Mobile chai-khanas are also common in Cameroon. The vendor will carry two buckets, one of hot water and the other filled with mugs and a large kettle. The tea is brewed from cloves and heavily sweetened with

This selection of Cameroonian specialties includes tilapia fish, samosas and plaintains, *ndole* with shrimp, chicken, goat meat, dipping sauces, and salads of tomatoes and onions.

BUSHMEAT

In Africa, the forest is often referred to as "the bush," and the meat from wildlife is called "bushmeat." Crocodiles, monkeys, antelope, squirrels, porcupines, and even elephants, gorillas, and chimpanzees are hunted for food. In rural areas of Cameroon— particularly in the southern forests—as well as in neighboring Congo, people may get up to 60 or 80 percent of their protein from bushmeat.

A significant uptick in bushmeat hunting resulted after mining and logging companies cleared roads into the dense forests back in the 1980s. Animals that had previously been protected by the impenetrable jungles were now accessible, and this has led to the increased endangerment of certain vulnerable species, such as gorillas and elephants. The concept of protecting endangered species can draw little sympathy or understanding from impoverished people. Guards in national parks face a constant threat of violence from angry villagers and poachers.

Not all bushmeat animals are endangered, however. Rodents make up a large percentage of the catch, and their populations are rather resilient to the pressures of hunting.

Aside from animal conservation issues, there is also a very real danger to people who eat bushmeat. Most don't realize that certain deadly diseases can be transmitted by handling, cutting the flesh of, cooking, and eating certain kinds of wild animals— particularly animals that are genetically close to humans, such as chimpanzees, gorillas and bonobos. The Ebola virus and HIV, the virus that causes AIDS, are two examples that are thought to have jumped from simians to humans this way. Gorillas may carry diseases such as simian foamy virus, chickenpox, tuberculosis, measles, rubella, yellow fever, and yaws. People have caught such diseases, and some have died. Even eating the meat of African squirrels and fruit bats may be dangerous.

Although the government of Cameroon has passed laws to regulate the bushmeat trade, the enforcement has been lax. Even city dwellers have a taste for bushmeat, and restaurants serve what their customers want.

sugar. Although cocoa and coffee are also produced in Cameroon, they are seldom drunk there. Apart from tea, the most common hot drink is Ovaltine, a nutritious chocolate-malt powder mixed with milk or hot water.

COOKING MEALS

In the countryside, cooking is done over a makeshift stove that consists of a small pile of charcoal between a few stones. Although traditional clay pots can still be found, more families nowadays use aluminum pots. A local stream is often used for washing dishes.

In cities and larger towns, many families have electric or gas stoves and running water. In rural settlements, people depend on the village well for their water. More villages now have a system to carry water from the well into the village.

A pounder, or large pestle, is the most common kitchen implement in both the countryside and in towns because it is essential for the making of fufu.

Food cooks in a pot over a fire in a traditional kitchen in Cameroon.

After the yam or other vegetable is cooked, it is mixed with water and pounded into a dough that is shaped as a soft ball.

STORED FOOD

The need to store food is more important in northern Cameroon than the south. In the southern forest regions, where rainfall is reliable, many crops can be grown throughout most of the year. In the drier climate of the north, farmers cannot always take the rain for granted; some years will have a long dry season followed by a short wet one, thereby reducing the quantity and quality of the harvest. Many villages have a common storage area where surplus food such as yams will survive for most of a year.

Even when enough food has been grown to feed the entire family, canned food is sometimes bought at the market to add variety to the menu

A street vendor sells fruit in Douala.

or when there is a special occasion. Canned sardines are a favorite among many Cameroonians.

A common sight at bus stations, and sometimes at makeshift stalls beside a main road, is a vendor selling fruit or vegetables. This is usually surplus food grown by the seller's family. Selling this fresh produce adds cash to the family pocketbook.

DRINKS

Most Cameroonians prefer to drink tea rather than coffee. Their favorite tea-drinking places are chai-khanas, local teahouses that also serve as meeting places for friends to exchange news and gossip. Besides teahouses, a common sight across Cameroon is a large truck making its way by road to remote villages to unload crates of soft drinks and Cameroon-brewed beer at local bars.

Palm wine is a popular alcoholic drink because it is locally made and inexpensive. A farmer may keep dozens of palm trees, planted at different times, so that there is a dependable supply of sap available year-round. A small cut is made in the trunk, and the sap is collected in a hollowed-out tube made from bamboo that is specially shaped to fit closely into the incision. This way, not a drop of the sap is wasted before it is poured into a large calabash, where fermentation soon starts.

INTERNET LINKS

https://www.africanbites.com/cameroon-food
This recipe collection features photos of many Cameroonian favorites.

https://www.sapiens.org/culture/bushmeat-public-health -cameroon
This article focuses on the health threats posed by eating bushmeat.

NDOLE

This dish of bitter leaf and groundnuts is often called the national dish of Cameroon. Boiled beef, goat, or smoked fish is often added to the stew. This simplified recipe substitutes spinach for the bitter leaf and peanut butter for the boiled raw peanuts, and uses shrimp as meat.

1 pound fresh spinach (about 10—
   12 cups raw) *or* 1 10-ounce package of
   frozen spinach
2—3 Tbsp cooking oil
2 large onions, sliced
2 Tbsp fresh ginger, grated
4—6 cloves garlic, chopped
1 cup natural-style peanut butter
1 cup beef broth, or more as needed
½ tsp each white and black pepper, salt

½ cup ground dried crayfish (optional, available at African or Asian ethnic grocers and online); alternatively, use a teaspoon or more of Thai fish sauce, to taste
½ pound raw large or jumbo shrimp, peeled

If using fresh spinach, wash and chop the leaves. Set aside.

Heat 2 tablespoons of oil in a large pot, and add the onions. Sauté over a medium heat until soft but not brown. Stir in the garlic and ginger, and cook about 1 minute more, or until aromatic. Add peanut butter and broth. Stir well. Transfer pot contents to a blender and blend until smooth. It should be the consistency of thick cream. If necessary, thin with more broth. Return the blended cream to the original pot. Bring to a boil, cover the pot, lower heat, and simmer for about 15 minutes. Add the greens and simmer, stirring frequently, just until spinach wilts. If using frozen spinach, cook until spinach thaws and cooks into the cream. Stir in the crayfish or fish sauce, if using.

In a separate frying pan, heat the rest of the oil, and sauté the shrimp lightly. Cook just until shrimp turns pink and is cooked through, about two minutes. Mix the shrimp into the greens. Serve ndole over rice, and/or with boiled or fried plantains and fufu.

FUFU

This Central African staple is usually made with cassava. Cameroonians also make a corn fufu, which is more like polenta. This recipe is what they call "water fufu."

Here are two versions. The cassava flour version is more authentic, though in Africa, many cooks begin with the raw tubers themselves, which is far more labor intensive. The second version is an adaptation for American cooks, using easily available materials. The taste will not be quite the same.

3 cups cassava or tapioca flour (also
    known in a more refined version as tapioca starch; available online, or in African or
    Caribbean markets. It may also be called "fufu powder.")

or

2 ½ cups instant mashed potato flakes
2 ½ cups baking mix, such as Bisquick

Bring 6 cups of water to a boil in a large pot. Add the cassava flour or the potato/baking mix combination. Stir vigorously with a strong wooden spoon. If using cassava, stir for 2 minutes over low heat, or until very thick. If using the potato/baking mix, stir for 10—15 minutes. You may need two people—one to hold the pot and one to stir.

In either case, if the fufu seems thinner than mashed potatoes, add more of the dry ingredients. The fufu should be very thick but must be stirred constantly to avoid lumping and burning.

Shape the fufu into balls: Fill a bowl with water and empty, but do not dry. Set aside. When the dough is stiff, scoop 1 cup into the wet bowl and shake until it forms into a smooth ball. Serve on a large platter alongside a soup or stew. To eat, pull off a bite-sized piece, make an indentation in the center with a thumb or finger, then use it to scoop the stew. Serves 6—8.

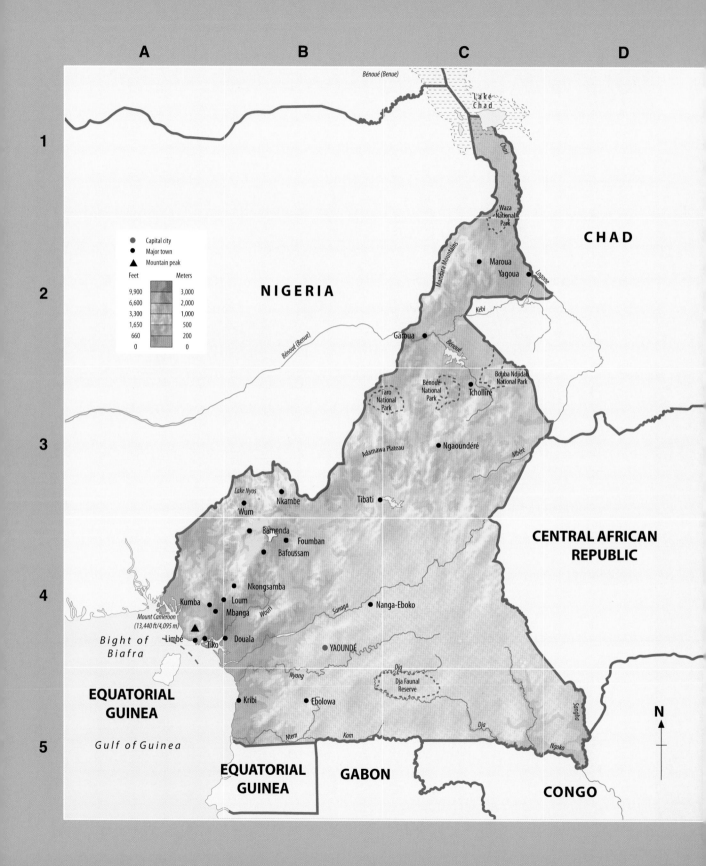

A   B   C   D

1

Bénoué (Benue)

Lake Chad

Chari

Waza National Park

2

CHAD

NIGERIA

• Maroua
Yagoua •

Logone

Kébi

Capital city
Major town
Mountain peak

Feet	Meters
9,900	3,000
6,600	2,000
3,300	1,000
1,650	500
660	200
0	0

Bénoué (Benue)

Garoua •

Bénoué

Bouba Ndjidah National Park

Faro National Park

Bénoué National Park

Tchollíré •

3

Adamawa Plateau

Ngaoundéré •

Mbéré

Lake Nyos

Nkambe •

Wum •

Tibati •

CENTRAL AFRICAN REPUBLIC

Bamenda •

Foumban •

Bafoussam •

Nkongsamba •

4

Kumba •
Loum •
Mbanga •

Wouri

Sanaga

Nanga-Eboko •

▲ Mount Cameroon
(13,440 ft/4,095 m)

Limbé •
Tiko •

Douala •

● YAOUNDÉ

Bight of Biafra

Nyong

Dja

Dja Faunal Reserve

Sangha

EQUATORIAL GUINEA

Kribi •

Ebolowa •

Ntem

Kom

Dja

Ngoko

N

5

Gulf of Guinea

EQUATORIAL GUINEA

GABON

CONGO

MAP OF CAMEROON

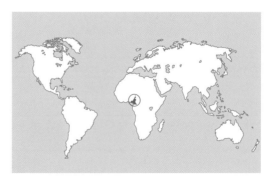

ECONOMIC CAMEROON

Agriculture
- Bananas
- Cassava
- Cocoa
- Coffee
- Corn
- Cotton
- Palm oil
- Rubber
- Tea
- Tobacco
- Yam

Natural Resources
- Cobalt
- Hydroelectricity
- Iron ore
- Nickel
- Timber

Services
- Airports
- Port

ABOUT THE ECONOMY

All figures are 2017 estimates unless otherwise noted.

GROSS DOMESTIC PRODUCT (GDP, OFFICIAL EXCHANGE RATE)
$34.99 billion

GDP PER CAPITA
$3,700

LABOR FORCE
9.912 million

CURRENCY
Central African franc (CFA)
US $1 = 579.44 CFA (June 2019)

UNEMPLOYMENT RATE
4.3 percent (2014)

POPULATION BELOW POVERTY LINE
48 percent (2011)

AGRICULTURAL PRODUCTS
cocoa beans, coffee, cotton

INDUSTRIES
agriculture, mining, manufacturing, trade, transport

EXPORTS
crude oil and petroleum products, lumber, cocoa beans, aluminum, coffee, cotton

EXPORT PARTNERS
Netherlands, France, China, Belgium, Italy, Algeria, Malaysia

IMPORTS
machinery, electrical equipment, transport equipment, fuel, food

IMPORT PARTNERS
China, France, Thailand, Nigeria

CULTURAL CAMEROON

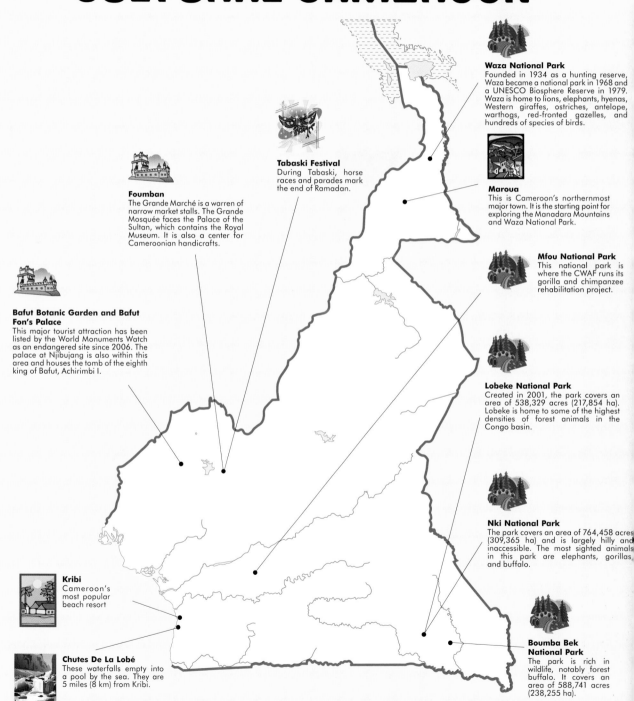

Waza National Park
Founded in 1934 as a hunting reserve, Waza became a national park in 1968 and a UNESCO Biosphere Reserve in 1979. Waza is home to lions, elephants, hyenas, Western giraffes, ostriches, antelope, warthogs, red-fronted gazelles, and hundreds of species of birds.

Maroua
This is Cameroon's northernmost major town. It is the starting point for exploring the Manadara Mountains and Waza National Park.

Tabaski Festival
During Tabaski, horse races and parades mark the end of Ramadan.

Foumban
The Grande Marché is a warren of narrow market stalls. The Grande Mosquée faces the Palace of the Sultan, which contains the Royal Museum. It is also a center for Cameroonian handicrafts.

Mfou National Park
This national park is where the CWAF runs its gorilla and chimpanzee rehabilitation project.

Bafut Botanic Garden and Bafut Fon's Palace
This major tourist attraction has been listed by the World Monuments Watch as an endangered site since 2006. The palace at Njibujang is also within this area and houses the tomb of the eighth king of Bafut, Achirimbi I.

Lobeke National Park
Created in 2001, the park covers an area of 538,329 acres (217,854 ha). Lobeke is home to some of the highest densities of forest animals in the Congo basin.

Nki National Park
The park covers an area of 764,458 acres (309,365 ha) and is largely hilly and inaccessible. The most sighted animals in this park are elephants, gorillas, and buffalo.

Kribi
Cameroon's most popular beach resort

Boumba Bek National Park
The park is rich in wildlife, notably forest buffalo. It covers an area of 588,741 acres (238,255 ha).

Chutes De La Lobé
These waterfalls empty into a pool by the sea. They are 5 miles (8 km) from Kribi.

ABOUT THE CULTURE

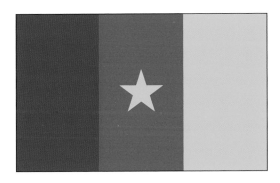

All figures are 2018 estimates unless otherwise noted.

OFFICIAL NAME
Republic of Cameroon

CAPITAL
Yaoundé

AREA
183,568 square miles (475,440 sq km)

POPULATION
25,640,965 inhabitants

MAJOR CITIES
Yaoundé, Limbé, Douala, Bamenda, Bafoussam, Maroua

OFFICIAL LANGUAGES
French and English

ETHNIC GROUPS
Cameroon Highlanders 31 percent, Equatorial Bantu 19 percent, Kirdi 11 percent, Fulani 10 percent, Northwestern Bantu 8 percent, Eastern Nigritic 7 percent, other African 13 percent, non-African less than 1 percent

MAJOR RELIGIONS
Roman Catholic 38.4 percent, Protestant 26.3 percent, other Christian 4.5 percent, Muslim 20.9 percent, animist 5.6 percent, other 1 percent, non-believer 3.2 percent (2005)

BIRTHRATE
35 births per 1,000 population

DEATH RATE
9.4 deaths per 1,000 population

INFANT MORTALITY RATE
49.8 deaths per 1,000 live births

FERTILITY RATE
4.58 children born per woman

LIFE EXPECTANCY
Total population: 59.4 years
Male: 58 years
Female: 60.9 years

LITERACY
Total population: 75 percent
Male: 81.2 percent
Female: 68.9 percent (2015)

TIMELINE

IN CAMEROON	IN THE WORLD
200–100 BCE Bantu tribes arrive from Nigeria.	
	600 CE Height of the Mayan civilization is reached.
	1000 The Chinese perfect gunpowder and begin to use it in warfare.
1520 Portuguese set up sugar plantations and launch the slave trade.	
	1558 Elizabeth I becomes the queen of England.
1600s The Dutch take over the slave trade from the Portuguese.	
	1776 US Declaration of Independence is written.
	1789–1799 The French Revolution takes place.
1884 Germans set up protectorate over Cameroon.	
	1914 World War I begins.
1916 British and French troops drive Germans out of Cameroon.	
1919 The London Declaration divides Cameroon into a British administrative zone and a French zone.	
	1939 World War II begins.
	1945 The United States drops atomic bombs on Japan. World War II ends.
1958 French Cameroon is granted self-government. Ahmadou Ahidjo becomes prime minister.	
1960 French Cameroon granted independence and becomes the Republic of Cameroon with Ahidjo as president.	
	1969 US astronaut Neil Armstrong becomes first human on the moon.
1972 Cameroon becomes a unified state and is renamed the United Republic of Cameroon.	
1982 Prime Minister Paul Biya succeeds Ahidjo as president.	
1984 Biya elected to his first full term as president. The country's name is changed to the Republic of Cameroon.	
	1991 Breakup of the Soviet Union takes place.

IN CAMEROON	IN THE WORLD
1992 Biya is reelected in Cameroon's first multiparty presidential election.	**1997** Britain returns Hong Kong to China.
1998 Cameroon is rated as the most corrupt country in the world by business monitor Transparency International.	**2001** Al-Qaeda terrorists stage 9/11 attacks in New York, Washington, DC, and Pennsylvania.
2002 Sovereignty of oil-rich Bakassi Peninsula is granted to Cameroon in an International Court of Justice ruling.	**2003** War in Iraq begins.
2008 Nigeria hands over Bakassi Peninsula to Cameroon, bringing an end to the volatile territorial dispute. Parliament amends the constitution to allow President Biya to run for a third term.	**2008** US elects first African American president, Barack Obama. **2009** Outbreak of H1N1 flu around the world.
2011 Biya wins in a landslide in disputed election.	
2013–2014 Boko Haram terrorists conduct incursions and kidnappings. Cameroon deploys 1,000 troops to the Nigerian border.	**2015–2016** ISIS launches terror attacks in Belgium and France.
2016 Government security forces shoot live ammunition at Anglophone protesters.	
2017 Anglophone regions call for independence from Cameroon. Violence ensues.	**2017** Donald Trump becomes US president. Hurricanes devastate Houston, Caribbean islands, and Puerto Rico.
2018 Biya wins a seventh term in an election marked by low turnout and voter intimidation. Government cracks down on separatists.	**2018** Winter Olympics are held in South Korea
2019 Switzerland offers to mediate in worsening Anglophone Crisis. Cameroon's women's soccer team protests loss to England in disputed World Cup game.	**2019** Terrorist attacks mosques in New Zealand. Notre Dame Cathedral in Paris damaged by fire.

GLOSSARY

Anglophone
English-speaking.

bush taxi
A cheap means of public transportation using cars, minibuses, and small trucks.

calabash
A large gourd, dried and used as a container, often carved and decorated.

camarões (CA-mah-row-es)
A Portuguese word for prawns or shrimp; the source of the name "Cameroon."

chai-khana (CHAI-kah-nah)
A teahouse set up in a taxi or bus station.

enstoolment
The coronation ceremony of a new chief; the seat of power is a beautifully carved stool.

fon (FON)
A local chief or king.

fondom
A hereditary chiefdom.

Frananglais
An informal language made up of a mixture of French, English, and pidgin words.

Francophone
French-speaking.

fufu (PHU-phu)
A doughy dumpling made from pounded corn, yam, or cassava flour.

jihad
The Islamic term for a holy war.

mancala
A popular pan-African, two-player, strategy board game. Also called *warri* (WAR-ree) and *awele* (a-wee-LEE).

mimbo (MEEM-boh)
A clay pot with a thick rim to prevent spilling, used for holding water or oil.

ndole (en-DOH-leh)
A dish of bitter leaf greens, shrimp, and plantains, often called Cameroon's national dish.

njama-njama (JAH-mah-JAH-mah)
A thick stew made from leaves of a vegetable similar to spinach.

pastoralists
People who live and work on farms, especially tending to animals.

pidgin English
A modified version of spoken English used in Cameroon and elsewhere among speakers who do not share a common language.

Ramadan
The ninth month of the Muslim year, when devout Muslims fast between sunrise and sunset.

shu-a (SHOO-r)
A food consisting of a pasty mixture made from pounded peanuts and flour, then fried.

FOR FURTHER INFORMATION

BOOKS

Homberger, Lorenz. *Cameroon: Art and Kings*. Seattle, WA: University of Washington Press, 2008.

Makuchi, and Isidore Okpewho. *The Sacred Door and Other Stories: Cameroon Folktales of the Beba*. Athens, OH: Ohio University Press, 2008.

Omatseye, Jim Nesin, and Bridget Olirejere Omatseye. *Going to School in Sub-Saharan Africa*. Westport, CT: Greenwood Press, 2008.

Sertori, Trisha. *First Peoples of Africa : Baka of Cameroon, Samuru of Kenya, Tuareg of the Sahara*. South Yarra, Victoria, Australia: Macmillan Library, 2009.

West, Ben. *Cameroon*. Bradt Travel Guide. 3rd ed. Guilford, CT.: Globe Pequot Press, 2011.

ONLINE

BBC News. "Cameroon Country Profile." https://www.bbc.com/news/world-africa-13146029.

BBC News. "Cameroon Profile—Timeline." https://www.bbc.com/news/world-africa-13148483.

CIA. *The World Factbook*. "Cameroon." https://www.cia.gov/library/publications/the-world-factbook/geos/cm.html.

The Commonwealth. "Cameroon." http://thecommonwealth.org/our-member-countries/cameroon.

Encyclopaedia Britannica. "Cameroon." https://www.britannica.com/place/Cameroon.

Human Rights Watch. "Cameroon." https://www.hrw.org/africa/cameroon.

Journal du Cameroun.com. https://www.journalducameroun.com/en.

Lonely Planet. "Cameroon." https://www.lonelyplanet.com/cameroon.

New York Times, Cameroon archives. https://www.nytimes.com/topic/destination/cameroon.

MUSIC

Bissaua, Emilio. *Cameroon: Songs, Hand Games and Lullabies*. ARB Music, 2019.

Bona, Richard, and Mandekan Cubano. *Heritage*. Qwest Records, 2016.

Dibango, Manu. *The Best of Manu Dibango*. Mercury Import, 2003.

Dipanda, Charlotte. *Un Jour Dans Ma Vie*. Phar Empire, 2018.

Kaïssa. *Looking There*. Makai Records, 2005.

Nyolo, Sally. *Studio Cameroon*. Riverboat, 2006.

FILMS

Chocolat. Orion Classics, 1988.

Minga and the Broken Spoon. Francophone Cinema, 2017.

BIBLIOGRAPHY

African Arguments. "Cameroon's Rising Religious Tensions." September 8, 2015. https://africanarguments.org/2015/09/08/cameroons-rising-religious-tensions.

Bax, Pauline. "Chinese-Built Port Evokes Dreams of El Dorado in Cameroon." *Bloomberg*, August 29, 2018. https://www.bloomberg.com/news/features/2018-08-29/china-stakes-its-claim-on-west-africa.

BBC News. "Cameroon Country Profile." https://www.bbc.com/news/world-africa-13146029.

Browne, Gareth. "Cameroon's Separatist Movement Is Going International." *Foreign Policy*, May 13, 2019. https://foreignpolicy.com/2019/05/13/cameroons-separatist-movement-is-going-international-ambazonia-military-forces-amf-anglophone-crisis.

CIA. *The World Factbook*. "Cameroon." https://www.cia.gov/library/publications/the-world-factbook/geos/cm.html.

Climate Home News. "Lake Chad Not Shrinking, but Climate Is Fuelling Terror Groups: Report." May 16, 2019. https://www.climatechangenews.com/2019/05/16/lake-chad-not-shrinking-climate-fuelling-terror-groups-report.

Dasgupta, Shreya. "Bushmeat Hunting Threatens Hornbills and Raptors in Cameroon's Forests, Study Finds." *Mongabay*, March 15, 2018. https://news.mongabay.com/2018/03/bushmeat-hunting-threatens-hornbills-and-raptors-in-cameroons-forests-study-finds.

Encyclopaedia Britannica. "Cameroon." https://www.britannica.com/place/Cameroon.

Freedom House. "Freedom in the World 2019: Cameroon." https://freedomhouse.org/report/freedom-world/2019/cameroon.

GAN Business Anti-Corruption Portal. "Cameroon Corruption Report." May 2017. https://www.ganintegrity.com/portal/country-profiles/cameroon.

Locka, Christian. "Cameroon Has Been Using Witchcraft to Fight Boko Haram." PRI, January 11, 2017. https://www.pri.org/stories/2017-01-11/cameroon-has-been-using-witchcraft-fight-boko-haram.

O'Donnell, Jecoate, and Robbie Gramer. "Cameroon's Paul Biya Gives a Master Class in Fake Democracy." *Foreign Policy*, October 22, 2018. https://foreignpolicy.com/2018/10/22/cameroons-paul-biya-gives-a-master-class-in-fake-democracy.

Owono, Julie. "The Martyrdom of Elephants: A Sad Tale of Greed." *Al Jazeera*, March 7, 2012. https://www.aljazeera.com/indepth/opinion/2012/03/201235112432745412.html.

Salkida, Ahmad. "Africa's Vanishing Lake Chad." UN, *AfricaRenewal*, April 2012. https://www.un.org/africarenewal/magazine/april-2012/africa percentE2 percent80 percent99s-vanishing-lake-chad.

UNAIDS. "Cameroon." https://www.unaids.org/en/regionscountries/countries/cameroon.

World Health Organization. "Cameroon: HIV Country Profile: 2016." https://www.who.int/hiv/data/Country_profile_Cameroon.pdf?ua=1.

INDEX

INDEX